LITTLE BOOK OF

PRADA

LITTLE BOOK OF
PRADA

LAIA FARRAN GRAVES

WELBECK

A stylist and journalist specializing in fashion and beauty, **Laia Farran Graves** has also worked for such publications as *Vogue, InStyle, Glamour, Marie Claire* and *The Sunday Times Style* magazine. Laia lives in London.

To Lucia

First published in 2012 and 2017 by Carlton Books Limited

This edition published in 2020 by Welbeck
An Imprint of HEADLINE PUBLISHING GROUP

37

Cataloguing in Publication Data is available from the British Library

ISBN 978 1 78739 459 9

Printed in China

MIX
Paper | Supporting responsible forestry
FSC
www.fsc.org
FSC® C104740

HEADLINE PUBLISHING GROUP
An Hachette UK Company, Carmelite House
50 Victoria Embankment, London EC4Y 0DZ

www.headline.co.uk
www.hachette.co.uk

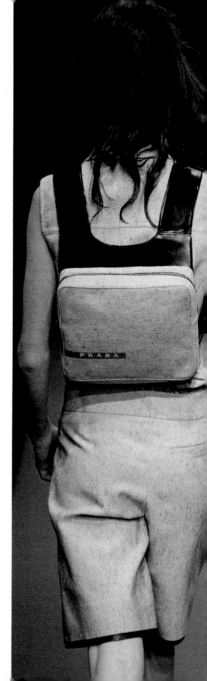

Contents

Introduction

The following pages tell the extraordinary story of Prada – a Milanese brand that began as a luxury leather goods company and was transformed into a multinational empire after the founder's granddaughter, Miuccia Prada, took over in 1978. This book explores Prada's visionary philosophy, along with the meteoric rise of the company and the global appeal of the label.

The first chapters consider Prada's aesthetic development, from the early accessories collections that culminated in the nylon tote in 1985 that changed the face of luxury accessories, to the most striking prêt-à-porter collections of recent times. We take a close look at key elements, highlighting the experimental and innovative way in which texture, fabrics and colour are used as a means to challenge our preconceptions of beauty.

Documenting Prada's crucial part in minimalism in its early years, this book reviews the company's progression and looks at the crucial role it played in the later return to femininity, strongly influenced by the silhouettes of the 1940s, 1950s and 1960s. At the same time, the ethos of the brand – a constant fusion of traditional values and techniques with ground-breaking modern ideas – is explored.

A chapter also discusses Miu Miu, Prada's diffusion line, and tracks its journey from the time when it first showed in Milan to the bold move to Paris Fashion Week in a quest to redefine itself in its own right. More recent collections are discussed and the essence of this quirky brand is outlined. Prada Men also features in a chapter that explores the label's menswear success and its own unique style. Other areas of the brand's involvement, such as the beauty industry, are also touched upon. The final section of the book highlights Prada's impressive engagement in the arts through the non-profit making Fondazione Prada, exciting plans for the future are unveiled and attention is focused on the unique contribution the company has made, and continues to make, to the art world.

Opposite Strong colours, simple elegant shapes and contrasting textures characterize the Prada brand's DNA.

Heritage

Italy's fashion capital is home to one of the greatest success stories of the twentieth century. The address of this grand establishment is Via Bergamo 21, Milan – Prada's headquarters.

The Prada story began in 1913, when Mario Prada and his brother Martino opened a leather-goods shop in Milan's lavish Galleria Vittorio Emanuele ll. This landmark nineteenth-century shopping arcade, with its glass roofs and mosaics, linked Piazza del Duomo with Piazza della Scala. The shop, known as Fratelli Prada (Prada Brothers), specialized in high-quality leather products and luxury items, and from the start became known for its excellence. Today, Prada has evolved from its origins as an intimate family business to a global fashion brand, led by Mario's granddaughter Miuccia. Prada currently has a presence in over 70 countries, with more than 600 shops worldwide. Beyond fashion, but in keeping with its creative ethos, the label has expanded into new areas through ventures such as its non-profit making arts organization, the Fondazione Prada, and its America's Cup Challenge Luna Rossa sailing team.

Back in 1913, using only the finest craftsmanship and materials, Mario Prada's company delivered luxury, style and originality, attributes that would become synonymous with the family name. Fratelli Prada created the classic Prada walrus leather case and imported steamer trunks from England. Luggage, handbags, beauty cases and a range of exquisite accessories, including walking sticks and umbrellas, were sold. By 1919, after just a few years in business, Fratelli Prada was appointed official supplier to the Italian royal family. This entitled them to use the House of Savoy coat of arms and knotted-rope design in their logo, and this logo is still used by Prada today.

Opposite The first Prada store opened in 1913 in Milan's Galleria Vittorio Emanuele ll. Mario and Martino Prada called it Fratelli Prada (Prada Brothers). From the start it reflected all the elegance, luxury and prestige that the brand is well known for today.

Miuccia Prada did not study design, pattern cutting or fashion, nor did she go to art school. Instead, after gaining a doctorate in political science from the University of Milan, she studied mime at the Piccolo Teatro di Milano in preparation for a career in acting, which she reluctantly had to leave to join the family business. Despite having what she describes as a dull childhood – she was made to wear plain

Previous page Milan's sumptuous Galleria Vittorio Emanuele II is home to Pradas's first store. The double arcade connects the Piazza del Duomo with the Piazza della Scala. It has an arching glass and cast iron roof – characteristic of nineteenth-century arcades – and spectacular marble and mosaic flooring. A majestic glass dome covers the central space.

Above Patrizio Bertelli had his own leather-goods business when he met Miuccia Prada in the late 1970s. The couple married in 1987, on Valentine's Day, and joined forces, transforming the family firm into a global brand.

Opposite A second Prada store opened in 1983 on Via della Spiga. It was just as luxurious as the first store, but with a more modern aesthetic.

striped dresses while dreaming of pink ones – she later took to wearing fabulous designer clothes, such as Yves Saint Laurent and Pierre Cardin, creating a very individual look. Her spirit and unmistakable sense of style have proved central to the reinvention of the Fratelli Prada business, taking it from a small family venture to one of the leading and most influential houses in the world of haute couture today.

Shortly after taking over the company, Miuccia met Patrizio Bertelli. Bertelli had his own leather goods firm and became her associate, focusing on the business side of things, as well as her husband. He has stood firmly by her side while she has devoted time to developing the brand's identity and direction. It was Bertelli who advised her to discontinue the English imports and to change their existing style of luggage – in 1979, the first line of nylon bags and backpacks was launched. Miuccia chose to use Pocone – a nylon fabric previously used by the company to line their trunks – because it fitted in with her love for everything industrial. This choice of fabric was technically challenging because nobody at the time was using it, and this made it more expensive to work with than leather. But Prada wanted to try something new and exciting that was functional and beautiful in – the fact that these bags were almost impossible to make simply added to the challenge. Perseverance paid off, and although the Pocone bags were not an instant success, they eventually became the brand's first commercial triumph.

For the next few years Miuccia learned everything there was to know about the business and soon she and Bertelli began to expand. In 1983 they opened a second store in Milan, on Via della Spiga, that maintained the attention to detail that characterized the original store, while displaying a modern aesthetic.

In 1985 Miuccia created one of the most iconic fashion items to date: the nylon tote handbag. Still experimenting with Pocone instead of leather, the fabric gave the bag an edge and made the design so desirable that counterfeit copies were manufactured worldwide. This created an even greater buzz that strengthened the brand: Miuccia had elevated the status of this nylon fabric from industrial to luxurious. The black bag, with its high price tag and discreet, but unmistakable, triangular metal logo, became a must-have for fashion editors all over the world and put Prada firmly on the map.

A line of footwear was also introduced at this time, followed four years later by the launch of Miuccia's first ready-to-wear collections. Initially, her minimalist, clean lines received a mixed response because they contradicted the big shapes and power dressing ethos of 1980s fashion, but a shift in aesthetics was taking place and within just a few seasons her unique look had become synonymous with chic. Prada as we know it today had established itself.

Above Prada continued to expand
by adding a shoe line to its existing
accessories collection in 1979.
Prada's quality and craftsmanship
continued to be an integral part of
each and every one of its designs.

The Early Years

In the 1980s, a number of established, luxury, handcrafted travel goods companies – Hermès, Louis Vuitton, Gucci and Prada – began to diversify and break into new ground with a focus on accessories, which created a platform for later fashion collections. But Prada took the brave move to also transform its image, adding a unique utilitarian and urban dimension to the long-established brand. This not only revolutionized the concept of luggage itself, but more importantly it gave way to a new aesthetic of contrasting fabrics, textures and clean lines, which became very much part of the label's signature and design identity.

At this time consumers were beginning to use accessories as status symbols and handbags were particularly in demand. Prada's timing in launching the nylon tote was perfect and the innovative use of Pocone, a tough industrial fabric, in a luxurious context was an intelligent move. It influenced the luxury market, crowning Prada the must-have label of its time.

Until the late 1980s Miuccia's focus stayed on creating the select accessories for which her grandfather's company had always been known. Although a new identity had been born, the production process remained unchanged. Handbags, for example, were designed and sketched, then plotted to create a stencil that was laid onto the fabric or leather. These sections were then skillfully cut out and sewn together by highly experienced workers. Beautifully constructed, each bag bore the original Prada emblem that had adorned the luggage of past Italian aristocracy.

Opposite Prada's innovative Pocone nylon backpacks cleverly fused luxury and attention to detail with a fresh industrial approach to accessories. The discreet Prada logo was kept low-key, making a statement that reflected the overall aesthetic of the times.

Expansion into Accessories

At the same time, Prada was also stamping its mark on another new venture: footwear. Their manufacturing methods might have been traditional, but the shapes and materials they used were truly ground breaking, capturing the public's imagination with their ingenuity and inspirational approach. Moulded rubber soles were combined with leather and other fabrics that had previously been reserved for sports and performance-wear, and had never been seen before in the context of luxury. These included technical fabrics, such as mesh and perforated leathers that gave an almost Aertex or piqué-like texture.

This page Using nylon to make backpacks was an unprecedented, bold move that revolutionized accessories in the 1980s. Despite using an industrial material, the quality and manufacturing process of the bags was second to none. Prada backpacks are still available today in a variety of colours.

PRADA
MILANO

This page and opposite The black
Pocone nylon tote was launched
in 1985, causing a stir in the
fashion world and placing Prada
firmly on the fashion map. Prada's
handbags, in all their variations,
have since become worldwide
objects of desire owing to their
quality and simple design.

This eccentricity and experimental approach to design, where modern and traditional techniques were fused together, resulted in a new perspective. Customers were now offered a delicate balance between classic and modern, which attracted creatives and fashionistas, as well as intellectuals.

In 1993 Prada was awarded the prestigious Council of Fashion Designers of America award for accessories. In the same year Miuccia also established the Prada Foundation (Fondazione Prada), whose objective was to provide patronage and showcase the work of

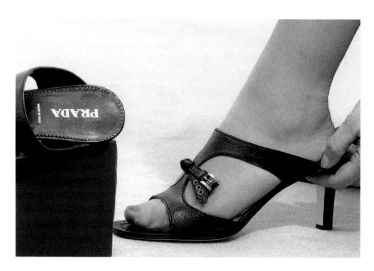

contemporary artists. Prada's penchant for art would also influence the brand's fashion collections, which often featured illustrations, Pop and Op Art imagery. Now all eyes were on Prada, whose mainline fashion collections were strongly coming into their own. New lines followed: Miu Miu in 1993, ready-to-wear clothes, shoes and accessories for men (also in 1993), Prada Sport (with its legendary "red line") in 1997, and the Prada eyewear collection (in 2000).

Above A footwear line, launched in the 1980sreflected the ethos of Prada by adding a modern dimension to classic designs. Some of the materials used may have been modern, but the manufacturing process remained traditional.

Opposite Prada's eyewear collection was launched in 2000 and sunglasses have played an important role in accessorizing the collections ever since. These orange goggles, featured in the autumn/winter show 2011, complete the outfit by adding a futuristic après-ski feel to the look.

Opposite and above Prada Sport,
the range dedicated to leisure,
launched in 1997. Characterized
by its unmistakable red line label
and simple, clean shapes, it
elevated casual and sportswear
to the luxury arena, both in its
clothing and in its accessories.

The Prada Aesthetic

When Prada was founded, the focus was on delivering tradition and luxury to Milanese high society in an opulent setting. By the late 1970s, when Miuccia took over as creative director and joined forces with her husband and business partner Patrizio Bertelli, change was inevitable if the brand was to survive. So they set their sights higher and raised the bar, creating a new Prada hallmark that has remained with the company through every stage of its development. The new ethos bound together an

"Always the problem with wanting to do structure is to do them in a way that still moves and is still comfortable, not really stiff."

Miuccia Prada

existing love of traditional values in an environment befitting the label's modern approach. Luxury and perfection coupled with a new avant-garde vision of the future found its expression in Prada's form of minimalism and was to become the brand's DNA.

This philosophy is reflected in all aspects of the business: from the way an item is designed, starting with a freehand sketch, to the company's deliberate decision to have employees of all ages working together. It is also present in the marrying of traditional techniques and craftsmanship, such as screen-printing and tie-dyeing with the latest cutting-edge technology. This can be so innovative at times that it is kept a company secret. By adopting this approach Prada has created a modern image of luxury that has pushed the boundaries and become unconventionally fashionable.

Opposite From the start, Prada's focus has been firmly on simplicity and clean lines to create beautiful yet wearable clothes. This voluminous, belted coat in nylon techno fabric, from autumn/winter 1990, was famously modelled by Helena Christensen in a dramatic black-and-white Prada advertisement.

The Minimalist Collections

One could argue that Prada's strength lies in its understated, quiet approach to fashion. The clothes are sexy and confident, but in a sophisticated and almost demure manner. Fashion reinvents itself constantly, just like art, reacting against previous trends and drawing on socioeconomic influences. It was not surprising then that after the 1980s, a decade of excess bursting with shoulder pads, neon colours, loud branding and logos, Miuccia's designs expressed a desire for simplicity, which was shared by designers such as Helmut Lang and Jil Sander. This new minimalism became Prada's trademark look and was welcomed with open arms.

To the untrained eye, the purist approach seemed almost too basic to work, but on closer inspection there was always a subtle, experimental twist. This may have escaped a large number of onlookers, but for those

Left The volume in this jacket from spring/summer 1992 is cinched with a narrow belt. The short, swinging length helps to create a defined, structured shape, as an alternative to the fluid hourglass.

Opposite A military influence is apparent in this high-neck, streamlined black ensemble for autumn/winter 1993, decorated only with highly-polished buttons and belt buckle. With a restricted colour palette and an emphasis on fabric rather than pattern or embellishment, Prada spearheaded the minimalist movement. Prada also launched the Miu Miu line in 1993, as the visionary sister label to the main fashion powerhouse.

in the know who appreciated and understood such subtleties, it added strength and value to the brand.

Prada's fluid lines and contemporary shapes provided a template that allowed Miuccia to work conceptually, giving her room to experiment with textures, fabrics, prints and colours. Her approach to design is a process whereby she surrounds herself with experts who can interpret her visionary ideas and bring them to life.

Opposite The spring/summer 1997 collection was feminine with 1950s influences. The cardigan, seen here in two shades of blue and worn as part of a twinset, would become a staple Prada piece that is both practical and elegant. The camel dress is simple in its shape, with a full skirt that adds fluidity to the garment as it moves.

Left Layering classic garments with accents of texture creates a modern, timeless and elegant look. In a subdued colour range of grey, black and white, this collection captures the mood of the early 1990s with its relaxed, simple and effortless beauty.

Above This white, summery hat looks like an ornate early 1960s swimming cap. Decorated with flowers, it is the perfect accessory for the spring/summer 1992 show, adding glamour, fun and a touch of irony in one simple accessory.

Opposite Strong patterns and clean lines are characteristic of Prada's designs. This dress, from 1992, has a provocative slit at the front that reveals matching shorts. The summery red-and-white stripes elongate and give structure to the outfit.

Opposite and above This outfit combines a piebald ponyhide jacket with a pair of blue silk, wing-print trousers. Contrasting patterns and original colour combinations are part of Prada's signature, creating garments that are innovative and exquisite. Prada's use of colour is often unorthodox and unusual in its combinations, but the results, such as the ochre, pale blue and brown used in the print for the trousers, are superb.

Colours, Prints and Textures

The label's quirky use of prints has been ongoing since Miuccia launched her first ready-to-wear collections. From the onset, the colour combinations were often unusual (for example, chocolate brown, lime green and white checks from spring/summer 1996), and the choice of prints were closely linked to the narrative running through each collection. In spring/summer 2000 the iconic print of lips and lipsticks added a hint of Pop art to an otherwise classic look.

Right Prada's design simplicity allows for interesting textures and colour combinations. Mustard yellow, olive green and powder blue were central to the spring/summer 1996 retro colour palette, which became known as the "Formica print" collection due to its references to 1960s kitchen vinyl patterns.

Opposite Miuccia Prada often revisits previous eras as influences for her collections. The pattern used here combines lime green, chocolate brown and white in a check design that harks back to the 1970s. The shape of the double-breasted coat and its short length is reminiscent of a 1960s miniskirt trend.

Overleaf Unusual textures, such as the peacock feathers on this skirt, shone in the spring/summer 2005 collection.

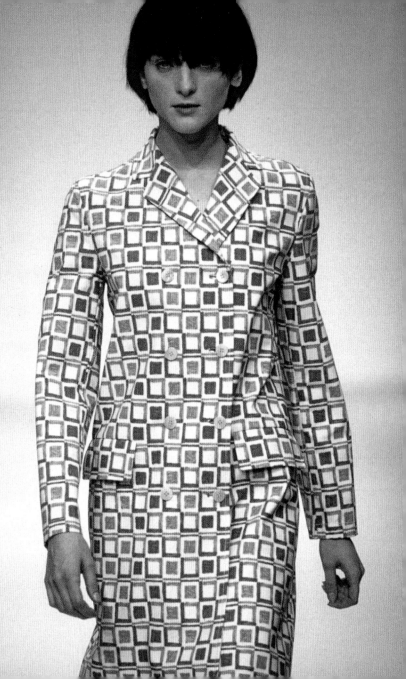

Autumn/winter 2003 saw the inclusion of striking William Morris prints in a winter-warming collection of tweeds, while in spring/ summer 2008 illustrator James Jean was commissioned to create a fantasy fairy print, adding a further dimension to an unexpectedly soft and flowing show (see also pages 108–113).

Miuccia also uses texture as a form of expression, sometimes in a provocative way, challenging preconceptions and taking elements out of context. Examples of this include a dress made entirely of fringing in spring/summer 1993, the oversize mirror detailing featured in spring/ summer 1999 (more traditionally found in Indian saris and sewn into the fabric like large sequins), and a skirt made out of peacock feathers for spring/summer 2005.

In autumn/winter 2008, Miucca repurposed the use of lace in a collection that almost single-handedly created an overnight trend: the lace revival (see pages 40–1). Black, brown, grey, ochre, gold, orange and light blue lace was not used as casual embellishment, but as the main fabric for dresses, shirts, skirts, trousers and even handbags in an otherwise austere collection. Never before had lace been seen in this light, away from its purely traditional decorative associations.

Left The spring/summer collection of 1999 showed some interesting oversized mirror detailing, sewn onto delicate garments, echoing the sequins found on traditional Indian saris and adding texture to an otherwise minimal look.

Above and opposite Defying tradition, lace was used in the autumn/winter 1998 to create complete garments and accessories rather than to embelish. The colours used were unusual for this type of fabric, and included black, brown, grey, ochre, gold, light blue and orange. The bright orange lace pencil skirt (above left), teamed with a camel lace shirt and orange sunglasses, is a great example of this unusual use of colour. Prada also used lace in this collection to make accessories. A black lace bag, with leather handles, matches black lace trousers (above right).

Opposite A military trend is present in many of Prada's collections. This brown coat from autumn/winter 1999 has two leather straps to fasten it at the front and leaves sewn all over it, adding texture and originality to an otherwise classic, no-fuss and utilitarian garment.

Above The shoes from the autumn/winter 1999 show were also decorated with foliage in leather appliqué, adding texture to a classic shape.

Left This full-length, fitted, textured dress in a stunning burnt orange hue, with fur trim over a chocolate brown top, played with texture and colour in autumn/winter 1993. Layering a rusty brown neckpiece adds to the overall look.

Opposite This dress, in an opulent golden shade of ochre, is from autumn/winter 1993. It is worn with an unbuttoned, chocolate-brown coat with structured, trimmed lapels. A purple hat and lace-up boots complement the outfit in an original colour combination.

Selling the Prada Look

Prada's past-meets-future ethos is also evident in its advertising campaigns, which have a strong and novel editorial narrative. Every campaign tells a carefully recounted tale in which the mood created and the model's expression become key. The clothes, which ironically become almost incidental, are part of a fantasy designed to appeal to consumers worldwide. The campaigns bring together the best production teams – headed by leading photographers such as Steven Meisel, who has shot the campaigns since 2004 – who interpret and convey Prada's modern vision.

Presenting a collection to the public creates yet another opportunity to showcase the essence of the brand. Prada's approach, no doubt influenced by Miuccia's time at the Teatro Piccolo, can at times be as theatrical as any major theatrical production. Since 2000 Prada has used a converted factory in Milan on Via Fogazzaro to host its shows. Time after time, the space is transformed through installations, screens and décor to fit with each collection's concept and deliver its specific

message. No detail is left to chance, from the design of the invitation and even the thickness of the envelope to when a choice of canapés is offered to the arriving guests. Everyone is left guessing and trying to join the dots, because although the Prada handwriting is unmistakable, it is also unpredictable. The lighting, music and seating plan are all part of a phenomenal production that transports the audience of fashion editors and buyers into a new world, daring them to suspend their disbelief and expect the unexpected.

Old and new, traditional and innovative… everything in Prada's world is touched by compelling and thought-provoking energy.

Above Prada uses every fashion show to convey the unique Prada experience to a select and influential audience. Spring/ summer 2011 combined colour, stripes and remarkable accessories – including striped fur stoles and shoes with three soles fused together as one – to produce a vibrant and summery show bursting with energy. The models' make-up harked back to the 1940s, with gelled, waved hair and silver eyeshadow.

Miu Miu:
Prada's Little Sister

In 1993 Prada launched a second label, which was named Miu Miu – Miuccia's nickname since childhood. This diffusion line was more affordable and directed to a younger customer, casting the Prada net still wider. Overall, Miu Miu has a very different energy to the mainline Prada collections: more youthful, vibrant, colourful, and at times sexy, eccentric and bohemian. It also places less emphasis on luxury and projects a greater sense of adventure. Although the two collections are clearly separate, there is a family resemblance and Miu Miu is often referred to as "Prada's little sister".

Miu Miu's triumph lies in its ability to encapsulate the effortless sense of cool that certain individuals seem to posess, throwing "any old thing" together and always looking fantastic. Often the styles – a skirt, a dress, a pair of trousers – appear simple at first sight, but their cachet is clinched by the original use of fabrics or prints.

From inception, Miu Miu captured the mood of the moment and created looks that were extremely wearable and accessible to fashion lovers. The label's identity – younger and less sophisticated than Prada – was reinforced by the eclectic advertising campaigns it ran. These sometimes used celebrities, such as Drew Barrymore, Chloë Sevigny, Katie Holmes and Vanessa Paradis, and in-vogue editorial photographers, including Terry Richardson, Juergen Teller, Mario Testino and the late Corinne Day.

The many faces of the Miu Miu girl contain infinite influences, making the brand impossible to pigeonhole. There are, however, some recurring themes that shape and define the label's personality.

"It's about the bad girls I knew at school, the ones I envied."

Miuccia Prada

Previous page For pre-autumn 2009, Miu Miu displayed playful elegance. This model is wearing a 1960s-inspired, embellished swing coat with wide arms and leggings with high heels.

Left The spring/summer 1999 collection was heavy on sports and leisure influences. This sleeveless, hooded top with a black zip is matched with very short shorts that add a quirky twist to an otherwise standard ensemble.

Opposite Military green is used here to create a dress with unexpected feminine detailing on the pockets and sleeves. In contrast, an orange belt bag creates definition and adds shape to the overall silhouette.

Plundering the Past

Revisiting past eras is something Miuccia Prada admits to having done since the very beginning of her fashion career – and it is also something for which she has become well known. Like a magpie, she has a way of collecting and bringing together retro highlights in a feminine and particularly girlie style. In "Portrait of Hailee" – the 2011 campaign shot by Bruce Weber – the collection is shot in *film noir* style, with a dramatic classical music soundtrack reminiscent of a silent movie. It features actress Hailee Steinfeld simply being herself – lying on the grass, sitting on a train track, daydreaming, laughing and eating pizza slices with her hands – and combines elements of vintage, such as beaded embellishments and calf-length dresses with modern touches, including coloured glitter shoes, to give an aura of upbeat nostalgia. This sentiment is also expressed through the elegance and sharp-suiting shapes of the 1940s, which are sometimes portrayed in an informal way (autumn/winter 2002 was a casual collection, which was feminine, pretty and playful with its use of delicate pale pink chiffon, striped T-shirts and wool skirts) and other times in a more mature, demure light (autumn/winter 2003 showed ankle-length classic dresses, skirts and smart hipster trousers worn with finishing touches of fur).

Opposite left The sharp, suited shapes of the 1940s were present in the autumn/winter 2011 collection. Sunglasses and fur tippets referenced Hollywood's glamorous Golden Age, reinforced by classic red lipstick.

Opposite right A further reference to the 1940s is seen in this elegant silhouette from 2002. Texture, in the form of quilting on the outfit, bag and boots, and colour add a modern dimension.

Above This double-breasted, military green coat, from autumn/winter 2002, is tied (not fastened) at the waist with a thin belt, softening an otherwise unisex garment. The models, with their side-parted hair and red lipstick, echo an austere wartime aesthetic.

Opposite Flashes of pink, yellow and green in a retro pattern on the model's top, lift what could otherwise be a fairly sombre outfit. The fur scarf and mohair sleeves create textures and layering, and the knotted belt and handbag complete the feminine look.

Preppy Chic

The simplicity of Miu Miu lends itself perfectly to the preppy look: neat, understated and with a focus on quality and classic shapes. When interpreted by Miu Miu, it has an almost-grown-up air, perfectly captured in the spring/summer 2000 show, "Almost a Lady", characterized by pleated skirts and baseball jackets. Spring/summer 2001 saw Prada take a modern twist to preppy, merging a 1950s shape with 1980s references such as drop-shoulder jackets to give an overall urban flavour. Big elasticated belts and full skirts were key, while the use of long socks with stilettos added a schoolgirl reference.

Another key feature of the preppy ensemble is the cardigan, which is present throughout the collections. Sometimes worn on its own, and often belted to accentuate the female form, it has become a staple Miu Miu garment, integral to the brand's aesthetic. Accessories such as hoop earrings, chain necklaces and wide, coloured Alice bands consolidate this look, reinforcing the air of innocence that Miu Miu so reassuringly delivers again and again.

Opposite Model Jacquetta Wheeler wearing a full red and black skirt, with a wide black belt that fastens at the front with a gold buckle. A simple grey knitted sweater with a high neck and grey socks paired with pointed heels add to the overall girlie look, so typical of Miu Miu.

Right Socks worn with high-heeled shoes add playfulness to the collection, and emphasize the youthful spirit of the brand. Here, colourful, geometric-patterned shoes stand out against a pair of plain, ribbed grey socks.

Left Bubblegum pink and black are the perfect combination for this preppy ensemble from spring/ summer 2000. The two-tone jacket, reminiscent of a 1950s bomber jacket, matches the pencil skirt and ladylike pink and black shoes.

Opposite Camel and light brown combine effortlessly here in a belted look that incorporates many of the key Miu Miu elements, including preppy styling, for 2002.

Sixties Scene

A-line dresses, Mary Quant flower references and platform shoes are all intermittently present in the Miu Miu universe, often in a way that incorporates the fitting, vibrant and lighthearted energy of 1960s fashion. With its narrow lines, neat minidresses and pretty skirts structured to create volume, the autumn/winter 2010 show was unusually sophisticated. Flower detailing embellished the fabric and high necklines with thin pussycat bows gave the look a sweet and up-to-date twist.

This trend, above any other, seemed to have captured the hearts of fashion editors: in August 2010 a very modern-looking 1960s-style dress from the Miu Miu collection featured simultaneously on the cover of *British Vogue*, *British Elle* and the US magazine *W*.

Never before had this occurred – a feat that was evidence of the brand's popularity and its ability to connect globally, which no doubt put a smile on Miuccia's face.

Opposite The autumn/winter 2011 collection was inspired by the 1960s. This orange A-line minidress, with silver flowers attached to the base, is accessorized with a pussycat bow and black shoes.

Right This lilac skirt, worn with a fitted black top with bow and a striking orange collar, is accessorized with a structured handbag, also in orange, and elegant high heels. The model's pulled-back hair adds to the severe composition of the look, which is softened by the feminine pocket detailing on the skirt.

Stars and Stripes

Often dresses on the Miu Miu catwalk are simple in their design. However, as with the mainline Prada range it is precisely this bareness that allows for prints to take centre stage. In a sense, the prints make the clothes special, something we see time and again in the work of Miuccia Prada. The 2008 autumn/winter print campaign, featuring Vanessa Paradis, is a perfect example. One of the shots is a close-up of the actress looking up, her head back and her eyes closed; you can only see the top of a dress, which has a strong pattern of orange, black, cream, chocolate brown and red. It's all about the girl and the print, a powerful image that exudes cool.

Overleaf right Autumn/winter 2008 was a collection inspired by jockey uniforms. The models wore "horse hoods" with their ponytails sticking out of the back, and had personalized leather initials sewn onto their clothes.

Overleaf left Nobody clashes prints better than Miuccia Prada. The spring/summer 1995 collection combined 1970s patterns in a variety of colours and styles. This retro shirt in lilac and browns blends effortlessly into a red, blue, brown and white skirt. The blue Alice band and fresh-faced make-up add a cool edge to the look.

Opposite Accessories are as much a part of the narrative of a Prada show as the garments themselves. This bag, with tan leather detailing, complements the retro-style dress by using a similar pattern in a slightly different colourway. By purposefully mismatching the patterns it creates a sense of contrast.

Retro prints resembling furnishing fabrics from the 1970s were seen in the 2005 spring/summer collection, a show that was all about simple shapes with bold and confident patterns in combinations of browns, ochres, greens and blues. Softer, prettier and more girly feminine prints are also prominent in Miu Miu: dresses with star prints in lemon and rose for 2006 and prints of animals for 2010. In 2011, stars, animals and lotus-flower prints were present in a glam-rock collection inspired by the current obsession with fame. Clashing of prints is another interesting format achieved either by combining two different prints or mismatching within a design. In spring/summer 2012 prints and patchwork appeared on boots, bags, dresses and a selection of gorgeous capes tied at the front or on the side with a thick, black ribbon. Worn with high-heel clogs and Western-style boots that added a folkie flavour to an otherwise Gothic collection, they stole the show.

Opposite left The spring/summer 2011 show was an exploration of fame, with glamorous and striking outfits. This silk satin shirt with silver latticework on the front is worn with a skirt featuring a star motif on the front. Fuchsia-coloured strappy heels add to the "rock chick" look.

Opposite right Miu Miu often uses pretty prints, such as this dark star design on a pale yellow background. The dress, worn here over a white T-shirt, is accessorized with sunglasses, long gloves and high heels, which add to the confident style that themed the spring/summer 2006 show.

Right The prints used in the spring/
summer 2010 collection were thought-
provoking and delicate in equal
measures. This outfit combines images
of white dogs on the black mini skirt,
with nude female figures on the soft
brown blouse and red collar.

Opposite A lotus flower print on
silk gave an oriental flavour to the
glamorous spring/summer 2011
show. A thin blue belt cinches the
dress to create a ladylike shape.

Miu Miu: Prada's Little Sister

Sexy Sirens

Miu Miu's approach to sensuous dressing takes many different guises and, as the brand evolves, it becomes ever present in collections through the styling and general attitude of the shows. In autumn/winter 2002, for example, high boots were worn with hotpants and overcoats, while in Spring 2008 extremely short dresses, evocative of French maids, *Alice in Wonderland* and *Playboy* bunnies, added a theatrical glow. The alluring and sexy advertising print campaign that accompanied the season, starred actress Kirsten Dunst and was shot by partners Mert Alas and Marcus Piggott, and featured a provocative 1950s-inspired pin-up look.

Opposite This outfit, from spring/summer 2012, shows an interesting combination of patterns in the patchwork-style dress and boots. The bag has a geometric pattern in pink, black and red, with a gold handle.

Right Two models backstage at the spring/summer 2008 show. The model in the foreground is wearing red lipstick to match her high-heeled shoes, a black and white puffball dress with white bloomer shorts, white cuffs and a black choker reminiscent of a *Playboy* bunny.

Overleaf left and right A multi-coloured, puffball minidress is beautifully accessorized with orange sunglasses while a delicate dress with a puffball skirt adds drama to a simple shape, both 2008.

After showing in Paris for the first time in autumn/winter 2006, a new chapter began for Miu Miu. As Miuccia herself commented, this was a way to make the diffusion line more special and important. Indeed, there is a palpable sense that this was the turning point for the brand, as if a newfound confidence had transformed the girls into young women. The venue chosen for the occasion was the famous eighteenth-century Lapérouse restaurant on Paris's Left Bank. Unprecedented touches of luxury accompanied this collection and its grown-up look was more sophisticated than anything previously shown. With red lips, short dresses and skirts, the models had a provocative air about them. Printed silks, long gloves and platform shoes with carved-out detailing on the heel proved to be complete showstoppers and the icing on the cake.

Opposite Shorts and high boots give a sensuous, but space-age, look to a 2002 utilitarian outfit of camel hooded jacket and shorts.

Right Autumn/winter 2006 was Miu Miu's first show in Paris, reinforcing the brand's stand-alone identity away from the mainline Prada collection. The models, who all wore matt red lipstick, looked confident and mature in the less girlie and more luxurious collection that included this silk dress with a still-life design photo-print.

Opposite Miucca's investigations into European history is reflected in the printed fabric of this simple dress from spring/summer 2009. Inspired by ancient Roman tiles or coins, a graffiti spray effect adds a modern touch.

Right and below The same bright pattern is used on the sleeveless dress and the sideways apron, which deconstructs the silhouette and adds structure to the dress.

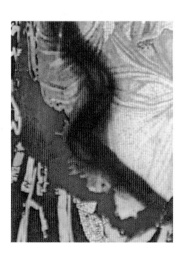

Menswear

In 1993, Miuccia Prada launched her first full menswear collection, which included footwear and accessories. Not only did the designs capture her mood, but season after season the collections kept Prada's brand identity running through consistently. A meticulously thought-out process is reflected in each garment, ensuring that beyond the shapes and silhouettes, elements of functionality such as pockets or the use of resilient fabrics play a vital role in the aesthetics of the line.

The mastery of contrasting and opposing elements is one of the strengths and signatures of the menswear range, something that is achieved in a number of ways. Prints range from 1970s-type patterns (autumn/winter 2003) to more abstract designs (spring/summer 2005) and candy-coloured florals (spring/summer 2012) and are all effortlessly combined with formal suiting to bring together both ends of the style spectrum. Unsurprisingly, texture is also used in an exploratory way and as a means of expression. High-twist nylon yarns normally employed in woven technical garments, for example, are utilized to create knitwear, while mohair knits – usually associated with womenswear – create interesting combinations, both visually and to the touch, with matt worked against high gloss or smooth against rugged, fur-like finishes. And in autumn/winter 2007 a series of garments (vests, tops and coats) in coarse, long-hair fabrics were shown alongside head-to-toe angora (hats, sweaters and leggings).

Unisex aesthetics and a look at duality were showcased in autumn/winter 2008, in a collection with a more conceptual approach. The runway presentation included garments such as bib-like tops, suggestions of jockstraps or skirt-like panels over trousers – Miuccia Prada at her most inventive and controversial.

Opposite Prada Men was launched in 1993, and included footwear and accessories. Over time, the collections have acquired a reputation for being meticulous in their execution and performance.

Overall tonal dressing reminiscent of the early minimalist ethos is something Prada has completely mastered over time in a way nobody else has done. In fact, it has become part of Prada Men's inherent individuality. Varying shades of navy, camel or grey may be worn with ease from head to toe, reflecting a lifestyle so understated it can be adapted to become one's own. And although fashion keeps reinventing itself, there are many classic, ageless shapes that can be loved and worn over and over, standing the test of time. Prada has established itself as a brand where a must-have item becomes a wardrobe investment, in particular the tailoring and outerwear garments that underpin the menswear range. Still today, it remains a highly aspirational brand and one that constantly challenges our idea of luxury.

Left Monotonal dressing is one of many distinctive trends favoured in the menswear line. Here, in the spring/summer 2006 collection, the model wears browns and greys in a classic suit, dressed down with silver trainers (sneakers).

Opposite A striking green V-neck jumper, worn over a shirt and tie, echoes a casual preppy look.

Opposite A particularly conceptual collection in autumn/winter 2008 looked at duality, and included double shirt collars, bib-like tops and hinted at jockstraps over the lower part of the shirts.

Right A striking coat with black and gold squares adds flair to a classic outfit of black trousers and tie worn with a white shirt.

Overleaf left The autumn/winter 2003 show prominently featured 1970s-style patterns. Here, a yellow, black and white tie clashes with a geometric-patterned shirt in white, blue and brown.

Overleaf right Prada expresses attention to detail through accessories. Here, a suit is worn with a multicoloured check trilby hat and a clashing tie.

Opposite Originality is key for this smart/casual outfit that features a summery shirt with a fish motif teamed with suit trousers, a belt and tie.

Right From spring/summer 2005, this abstract printed shirt in orange, brown, white, green and yellow is worn with tailored trousers and colourful trainers (sneakers).

Opposite The autumn/winter 2007 Prada menswear collection explored texture and colour in its knitwear and outerwear. Here we see a striking black fur coat worn over a pristine white shirt.

Above Badger-fur-covered crash helmets in autumn/winter 2006 lighten the show and add texture to an otherwise classic collection. Quilted, leather-trimmed shirts and cashmere knitwear slung over shoulders were standouts from the collection.

Accessories

Accessories also break the mould of what is considered standard, not only for their design (spring/summer 2011 showed lace-ups with a compressed three-tier base of leather, espadrille and trainer-soles), but also in the way they are combined with the rest of the outfit. Suits were worn with silver trainers (spring/summer 2006) and fur-covered crash helmets (autumn/winter 2006) added a touch of humour to the show, lightening the mood.

Men's mainline accessories still retain the brand's trademark styling of confident, clean, organic lines and provide the must-haves of the season by mixing tones and textures, such as perforated leather, ostrich skin or high polish with matt finishes. The brand's approach to elegance and sophistication is often coupled with a touch of sports detailing and comfort is never compromised.

Right Accessories are an important part of the Prada Men style. Classic suiting is jazzed up with sunglasses and a fur-covered helmet.

Opposite Spring/summer 2012 was full of golf references, from shoes to flat caps. Nylon bags and leather folders provided finishing touches.

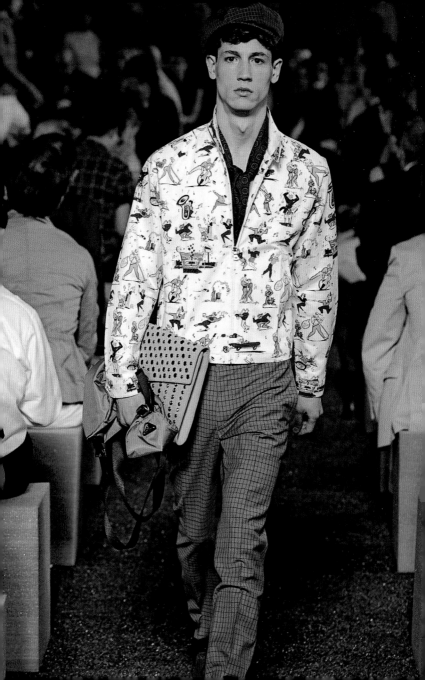

The Prada Man

The spirit of Prada menswear comes alive in the shows and campaigns. Just as in womenswear, the male models cast by the House of Prada are often not conventionally good-looking, but are chosen because they encapsulate the feel of the time. This reinforces the idea that Prada is not merely about frivolous beauty and adds depth to the narrative of the story.

In many cases models are chosen at the beginning of their careers, as if Miuccia had a sixth sense that enables her to discover the face of the moment, and they rocket them to fame soon after. The same applies to Miuccia's brilliant choice of celebrity faces – among them Tim Roth, Joaquin Phoenix and Tobey Maguire – that represent Prada's idea of modern masculinity, removing the focus from bravado or a macho image.

Opposite left This vibrant blue blazer is worn with a striped black, red and white shirt. The outfit is accessorized with sporty, wrap-around sunglasses worn around the neck.

Opposite right Glasses and sunglasses have been a key accessory in the Prada look since their launch in 2000. These wraparound glasses add a sporty element to this preppy outfit.

New Millennium Collections

In the run-up to the new millennium, fashion began to draw on past references and the first decade of the twenty-first century saw a return to femininity and ladylike elegance. Prada was a key player in this shift in aesthetics.

The rise of the Internet changed the pace at which the world communicated and fashion became more fluid and fast-changing. High-street retailers established themselves in the marketplace with the concept of live collections that could be designed, manufactured and sold within days. To ensure their position in the market, luxury brands highlighted their heritage and quality values. Prada, following a compelling desire for reinvention, went one step further in creating an ever-changing modern and classic image that was to become its blueprint and embodied a no-fuss functional identity.

Opposite Miuccia Prada, the woman whose vision and creative force reinvented the House of Prada, greets the audience after a fashion show in 2007.

The Ladylike Collections

Elsewhere in the fashion world, military garments, the grunge look and a return to vintage were strong influences and although Miuccia Prada incorporated some of these elements in her designs – she is a self-confessed uniform lover – the focus on exploring and reinventing the ladylike formula remained, characterized by belted shapes over pencil or full skirts, complete with high heels and the obligatory structured handbag.

Prada's spring/summer 2000 collection was launched to great applause. Presenting a refined silhouette and using a colour palette that included camel and white with accents of lilac and yellow, the collection was beautifully accessorized by high heels and handbags, showcasing the company's complete product range. Polo necks were styled with fitted skirts and warm colour combinations, together with "lips and lipstick" motif prints that ensured the austerity typifying these garments also had an edge. This clear-cut silhouette was to resurface over the seasons, redefining elegance and keeping the fashion audience on its toes, wondering what the next twist would be.

Almost a decade later, in the autumn/winter 2009, this same shape returned, but this time with an accompanying back-to-basics approach and an air of starkness that mirrored the bleak financial times. Tweed, pencil skirts and fabulous fabrics made for a winning formula that ticked all the boxes, as Prada came full circle in the quest for continuous reinvention.

Opposite left A white, fur scarf, with accents of black, worn with a fur gilet adds volume and texture to a feminine outfit.

Right A fur collar, tied at the front, accessorizes this belted yellow patterned dress, which is worn with peep-toe heels, all of which evoke a 1940s flavour.

Opposite This pencil skirt, teamed with a lilac cardigan and a scarf, creates the ladylike silhouette for which Prada has become known. The spring/summer 2000 collection oozed this kind of understated, prim and polished style.

Left A camel jumper over a yellow shirt, worn with a belted brown pencil skirt, combined seamlessly in spring/summer 2000 to create a classic feminine look.

Opposite The iconic lipstick print on the fabric of this skirt was featured in the ad campaign for spring/summer 2000. Here, the skirt is worn with a fitted cardigan and matching shoes and bag.

Above and below The shoes from the spring/summer 2000 collection sported the iconic lip print and love hearts, creating a fun and feminine look.

Conceptual Collections

Another key ingredient in Prada's anthology is the conceptual aspect of the work, which reflects Miuccia's love of ideas and ability to make us question our preconceptions. It explores interesting shapes and unusual concepts, such as see-through outerwear (autumn/winter 2002), which are often fused with historical references. One of the most striking displays of intellectual expression is the autumn/winter 2004 collection, a unique show with Prada's ethos written all over it. Anchored in elegance, it combined references inspired by nineteenth-century paintings from the German artist Caspar David Friedrich, with video-game graphics. Miuccia spent hours watching video games to capture the mood of the virtual world and successfully turned this concept into wearable clothes: T-shirts with robot appliqué were worn with full skirts; coats and skirts were made from computer-generated printed fabric; and classic bags were accessorized with robot key-chains made from industrial components. In keeping with the essence of her signature elegance, the show brought together high and popular culture in a journey through the ages.

Left This conceptual, see-through mac with black piping made a statement in 2002. The raincoat becomes opaque when wet.

Opposite For autumn/winter 2004, Prada presented a collection that combined references inspired by the nineteenth-century German artist Caspar David Friedrich with video game graphics. This pencil skirt, jumper and open coat, with a high belt tied to the side and featuring an unusual print, show how the achieved look was both elegant and original.

Overleaf left and right Prada introduced some fun in autumn/ winter 2004 by accessorizing classic bags and belts with robot key-chains made from industrial components. This was a great example of past and present coming together as one.

Colour Splash

Prada's pursuit of the unusual is always apparent in Miuccia's experimental colour schemes, which over the years have caused a few raised eyebrows – sometimes for being overly mute, other times too bright, or for matching colours that theoretically shouldn't go together. Even when the collections are kept fairly monochrome they usually contain dashes of unexpected colour, even if it's just the accessories. A particularly strong collection, spring/summer 2003, incorporated vibrant colours – lime green, orange and pink – in a contemporary display of Prada's much-loved 1960s shapes and accessories, with some

Left This sleeveless green dress encapsulates the simplicity of Miuccia's masterly lines.

Opposite left Spring/summer 2003 incorporated vibrant colours, such as this orange skirt and pink top – worn here with sunglasses to add a sports chic element to the outfit.

Opposite right The spring/summer 2005 show introduced tall, crocheted cloche hats, chain and beaded necklaces and adorned fabrics. This plain grey shirt is given a lift with a necklace of yellow, red and navy textured beads and has embellishments attached to the shirt pocket.

sports-chic elements thrown into the mix and flat sandals gracing the catwalk. The spring/summer 2005 show introduced bright feathers in skirts and dresses (see also page 38); also tall, crocheted cloche hats, chain or beaded necklaces and embellished fabrics. Lively short dresses, casual shoes and Caribbean influences all came together under a reggae soundtrack. More colour was seen in spring/summer 2007, when rich jewel tones shone in a feminine show with shapely lines. Here, the girls wore belted frocks in reds, purples, greens and blues with contrasting coloured turbans that were reminiscent of 1940s headdresses from the Golden Age of Hollywood.

Prints and Patterns

Prada's brilliance is also reflected in Miuccia's choice of print and pattern, which sometimes includes a hint of irony – in spring/summer 1996, for example, she used 1970s-inspired retro prints (see pages 36–37). Other collections, such as autumn/winter 2003 showed sublime taste, which included spectacular William Morris prints in a wintry show that included accessories such as trilby hats and gloves.

Some of the most talked-about work to date was featured in 2008. In the spring/summer show, Miuccia collaborated with illustrator James Jean to produce a print that integrated elements of a graphic novel with surreal and romantic notions, as well as sci-fi elements. Ever evolving, yet always true to her core style, the result was a "fairy-tale" collection, where delicate silks blended with bold Art Nouveau influences. The print was used as a backdrop mural and as a prominent feature in the season's advertising campaign; it also became one of many wallpapers displayed in Epicentre stores. Afterwards, Jean and Prada collaborated in a short illustrated film, *Trembled Blossoms*, which was presented at the New York Epicenter during Fashion Week.

Opposite The autumn/winter collection of 2003 included this stunning, green William Morris print dress.

Left The clashing of prints is achieved beautifully in this autumn/winter 2003 ensemble. Here a classic Argyle pattern in green, grey and black is worn with a 1970s-inspired short-sleeved shirt.

Soon Prada's popularity had reached an unprecedented high, and outside the catwalk the label had come to mean much more than fashion. Indeed, it had become embedded in current popular culture. The year 1998 saw the launch of the iconic TV series *Sex and the City* (1998–2004) featuring four glamorous, fashion-loving New Yorker female friends. The main character, Carrie Bradshaw (played by Sarah Jessica Parker), was frequently dressed in Prada or seen carrying a Prada shopping bag. In 2008 *Sex and the City*, the film, was released, followed by a sequel in 2010. Another huge box-office hit acclaimed by fashionistas worldwide was *The Devil Wears Prada* (2006), a romantic comedy staring Meryl Streep and adapted from Lauren Weisberger's novel, which reinforced the label as a household name. Prada garments were used extensively in the movie and it is estimated over 40 per cent of the shoes worn by Streep in the film are by Prada.

In the music industry, urban artists not only started to wear Prada clothes – particularly rap and hip-hop stars – but they also began to "label drop" in their lyrics as a means of depicting success and status. Among them were Jay-Z ("Girl's Best Friend", 1999), Hip Hop Dub Allstars ("I Just Wanna Love You [Give It 2 Me]", 2000), Enur ("Ucci, Ucci", 2008) and Fergie ("Labels Or Love", 2008).

Opposite For the spring/summer 2008 show Prada collaborated with illustrator James Jean to produce a print for the collection. Here, a green silk dress is worn with contrasting yellow and black tights and Art Nouveau-style shoes.

Overleaf left This ethereal, lime green silk top, with matching trousers, gives the model an almost fairy-like quality as she walks down the catwalk. A waved neckline adds to the sense of fluidity of the outfit.

Overleaf right Illustrator James Jean produced a backdrop mural for the catwalk show and designed wallpaper that was displayed in the Prada Epicenter stores. Jean also created a four-minute, animated film called *Trembled Blossoms* that was shown at the New York Epicenter. A later installment featuring the same nymph-like protagonist, *Trembled Blossoms Issue 02,* was later shown at the Tokyo Epicenter. The print was used in handbags, shoes and packaging.

Above A brown tie-dye dress, accessorized with a black belt that emphasizes the waist and a neckerchief in a colourful print.

Above left This breathtaking sleeveless dress, in graded shades of grey, cream and olive green, is ruffled to create texture and shape.

Opposite The spring/summer 2004 show emphasized traditional crafts, which included dip-dye and tie-dye techniques. The print on this dress, worn open and tied with a belt, has tribal influences.

A New Decade

The Prada collections in the years since 2010 have displayed a new energy and boldness that perhaps only comes with experience. Retaining its signature style throughout, the shows have shone brighter, capturing the attention of a global audience in an unprecedented way. This success has in turn become a powerful new strength, so influential that the trends it features, from ladylike clothing to prints or faux fur, have instantly risen to the top of the fashion charts. It would almost seem that Miuccia Prada has a crystal ball telling her exactly what people want and when they want it.

"I am always researching new ideas on beauty and femininity and the way it is perceived in contemporary culture."

Miuccia Prada

Opposite Oversized sequins that look like fish scales glisten in the autumn/winter 2011 show. Oversized orange sunglasses and boots in snakeskin and suede that look like shoes worn with socks, add glamour to the look.

Overleaf left An inspired 1950s silhouette took centre stage in the autumn/winter 2010 show. This outfit contrasts two different prints and is accessorized with gloves, a handbag and bow-detail shoes that accentuate the femininity of the collection.

Overleaf right Black ruffles over the bust area of this red dress add volume and reinforce the feminine hourglass shape. Long socks and red matching shoes and knitted handbag are the perfect finishing touches.

Mad Men's Women

For autumn/winter 2010 we saw a return to the glorious femininity reminiscent of Prada's earlier collections from the start of the century. This time, however, the ladylike style was strengthened by a slightly redefined silhouette that was curvier and emphasized the bust as much as the waist. The new look also included strong, large prints with a retro air about them in stunning faded browns, blues and reds. Frills and ruffles added volume to the bust area and there were some almost fetishistic touches, such as the combination of rubber with knitwear or open-toe stilettos worn with generously thick socks. Hair was worn in a dramatic beehive with a knitted band, exposing a clear face with little make-up and accessories accentuated the ladylike theme – gloves, skinny belts with bow detailing, small or medium handbags, high heels (pointed, rounded, strappy) and cat's-eye glasses that could easily have belonged to an eccentric, 1950s, sexy secretary. It was a strong collection that reflected the popular TV series of the time *Mad Men* (2007–2015), with its feminine curves and 1950s styling. Very much designed for real women, it brought with it a sense of fun and flirtatious beauty.

Prada Goes Bananas

The following show, spring/summer 2011, had such an impact worldwide and was so influential that it can, to a large extent, be considered responsible for some of the main trends that season: strong prints, bright colours and colour blocking. Simple lines in above-the-knee suits, separates and dresses allowed for an unparalleled burst of colour. The models' make-up featured silver eyeshadow and hair gelled in 1920s-style waves.

Plain bright orange, electric blue and emerald green frocks opened the show with a vibrant energy that was also present in a series of striped designs. These stripes were seen on oversize hats, handbags, skirts, tops, stoles, dresses and jackets – sometimes alone and at other times part of a larger, more ornate design or print. The accessories were unforgettable, their message loud and clear: from large picture hats to the intricately exquisite platform braided shoes and swirly detailed sunglasses, which have been aptly named "minimal baroque".

There was also a touch of humour running through this collection, perhaps best typified by Miuccia's use of the "banana print" (green or yellow bananas on a dark background) that introduced a tropical ease and flamboyance into the show – a joke shared by many, including *Vogue* editor-in-chief Anna Wintour, who has been spotted wearing at least three different versions. Even banana earrings were added to the collection before it hit the stores after Miuccia was seen sporting a pair on the day and they became the talk of the show.

Top With hair styled in slicked-down finger waves, feet elevated on striped espadrille wedges, and walking to a mix of tango and flamenco music, the models at the spring/summer 2011 show evoked a Latin American vibe. In keeping with this, monkey and banana prints were used on flounced Baroque-print rumba skirts and bowling shirts.

Bottom Miuccia Prada, the designer who made black nylon chic, takes a bow wearing a pair of banana earrings.

Opposite The influence of the American dancer, singer and actress Josephine Baker is impossible to ignore. In this 1927 lithograph by Paul Colin, Baker is shown performing the Danse Sauvage at the Folies Bergères, wearing a skirt made of artificial bananas. Baker's iconic performance style, voice and costumes made her hugely successful, and by 1963 she was one of the highest paid performers in the world.

Opposite This dress, in black, white and blue stripes, paved the way for the colour mismatching and print-clashing trend that followed that season.

Above left Platform shoes take a new turn with these three-tiered soles made of fused leather, espadrille and rubber. A compact handbag completes the look.

Above right A wedge is given added height by fusing several soles together. Here, the blue rubber sole matches the classic Prada handbag.

Overleaf left This low-slung outfit is strongly influenced by 1920s flapper dresses. Its geometric design also resembles Yves Saint Laurent's colour-block Mondrian dress from 1965.

Overleaf centre Pearlescent sequins have a shimmering fish-like effect. The models held onto their handbags tightly at this show, which became a much talked-about point.

Overleaf right A belted coat becomes an extraordinary bird-like garment with the addition of gold sequin front panel and fur trim on the sleeves.

For autumn/winter 2011 the mood remained playful but more seductive, with an added injection of glamour in an exciting collection of 1960s-inspired short shapes, dropped-down waistlines from the 1920s and knee-high boots with a curved heel.

The girls looked young and innocent. Clutching their handbags tightly, they wore little make-up, with blush used both on the cheeks and on eyelids. In contrast, reptile skin featured in coats, bags, shoes and boots, some of which were particularly striking – especially the two-tone coloured boots that looked like long socks under Mary Jane shoes. Oversize resin sequins resembling fish scales glistened on the dress, adding an aquatic feel. Fur and fake fur were also explored, particularly in outerwear – which became a big trend in autumn/winter 2011. Accessories added sublime finishing touches to a futuristic image with eyewear that looked like oversize goggles and bonnets resembling swim or aviator caps with straps under the chin, in python, wool cloth and fur. Combined, these unlikely influences created a mesmerizing image of rare beauty and also set the tone for a number of new trends, including textured outerwear, 1960s shapes and shimmer.

Women and Car Engines

The spring/summer 2012 show was a captivating, 1950s-inspired, candy-coloured collection titled, Women and Car Engines, with automobile references in accessories, garments and prints. Once again a new set of contradictory elements came together in Prada's trademark ladylike look, successfully portraying a retro-bourgeois style with accents of vintage. The venue was made to look like a car park or garage, with pink paint stains on the floor that might suggest a recent spray job. Cartoon-like cars made from foam provided some of the seating. Models emerged wearing natural make-up, with pale pink lipstick and side-parted hair that was loosely waved and tidy.

The colour spectrum was delightfully soft and clean, and included pastel shades such as pale pink, yellow and blue, as well as stronger hues like turquoise, bottle green, deep red or bubble-gum pink. It was a collection of dresses (many in flowing chiffon), skirts (pleated and pencil-shaped), floaty blouses and cotton tube-tops, which also featured structured, embellished coats and glamorous satin swimming costumes, panelled and shaped to enhance the hourglass figure.

The accessories that stole the show, however. Vintage-inspired earrings, bracelets and necklaces featuring an adornment of roses were reminiscent of heirlooms handed down through the generations – this collection inspired Prada to launch their first jewellery collection in 2012. In an otherwise classic look, some of the bags had studs as embellishment while others bore pictures of cars. Also in keeping with the theme, some of the shoes had cutout flames on straps and small tail-fin lights on the heel, adding a super-hero quality and strength to an otherwise sweet portrayal of elegance.

So, what will come next? We have all come to expect the unexpected from Prada, so there are sure to be more surprises in the future.

Left and above The 1950s-inspired show was all about "Women and Car Engines". The light blue top, with its car print, was worn with a leather pencil skirt with a pink Cadillac-style car on the front. The shoes from the spring/summer 2012 collection were sensational. The ones seen here had cutout flames on the side-straps, and small tailfin lights.

Overleaf The cartoon car print was used for this pastel coloured dress, which is cinched at the waist and falls just above the knee.

Opposites Attract

The autumn/winter 2016 collection juxtaposed themes like no other before. In a deconstruction of a traditional linear narrative (also present in the autumn/winter 2013 and spring/summer 2015 collections), this show combined a number of looks and styles that – at a glance – would appear to have been thrown together but instead, of course, had been meticulously curated one by one. The backdrop to the show was a dark, wooden set with a balcony on which a few candles flickered, evoking a faraway place and time.

The show began with tailored jackets and coats worn with corsets over them as belts, and argyle tights matched with lace-up boots. We then saw military-inspired jackets, which were at times worn with full-length feminine 1950s-style dresses in exquisitely delicate gilded silk. Then there were big tailored jackets with fur trims and embellishments on dropped sleeves, deconstructing the classic silhouette. There were also pattern-clashes worn throughout with lots of accessories layered on at once – such as necklaces, trinkets (personal diaries and keys) long knitted gloves, stark white sailor hats, belts and bags (models sometimes wearing more than one as if thrown together). Fabrics were also varied throughout the presentation: leather, fur, velvet, silk, brocade, cotton, nylon, but they all came together in a collection that seemed to embrace a number of elements or aspects of the journey that is womanhood, almost as if in a search of a woman's own identity.

In Prada's own words: "We need to understand who we are now... Maybe it's useful to look back to the different characteristic moments, difficulties, love, no love, pain, happiness, different kinds of women: sexy, boring, traveller... So this was the main concept."

The show also seemed to communicate a sense of uncertainty on a more symbolic level: the pristine white sailor caps reminiscent of World War II, and the overall image of the traveller who wears all her possessions at once, fleeing or moving on, echoing the "vagabond" woman – perhaps mirroring the general unpredictability that is felt in today's world of global politics.

Left Autumn/winter 2013: two silhouettes, two textures, two lengths and two colours produce a unique, unmistakably Prada, asymmetric dress.

Above This two-tone sublime clutch bag from spring/summer 2015 is worn against an exquisitely delicate frayed shirt and skirt with no hemline.

Opposite Autumn/winter 2016's "vagabond" collection effortlessly combines textures, patterns, colours, accessories and styles.

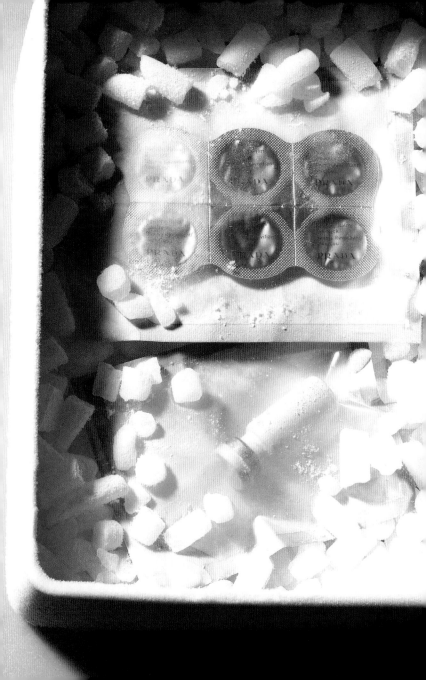

Beauty and Fragrance

Prada's launch into the cosmetics industry reinforced the lifestyle aspect of the brand, allowing it to reach out to a far wider audience and making it more accessible to the general public.

The first launch, in 2000, was Prada Beauty – a line of cosmetics that shared the label's identity in a minimalist, yet futuristic packaging. Its unique selling point was that it presented premium products in one-application blister packs that were ideal for travel. Then, in 2004, the first women's fragrance was introduced. The debut scent – created by Max and Clement Gavarry in colaboration with Carlos Benaim – has been described as a modern classic. With top notes of bergamot, orange, rose and patchouli, it carried all the beauty and simplicity associated with the Prada name and was presented in a simple, rectangular glass bottle with the lid to one side – an eye-catching design that has since been used for a number of Prada fragrances, including L'Eau Ambrée and Prada Tendre.

Opposite and above In 2000 Prada launched a beauty and skincare line. It was uniquely presented in single-application packs and the overall design of the packaging was clean, futuristic and minimal.

The first fragrance for men, launched in 2006, was a timeless, yet contemporary scent: rich, clean and characterized by a soapy smell reminiscent of an old-fashioned barber's shop. Others in the men's range include Infusion d'Homme, Infusion de Vetiver and more recently, Amber Pour Homme Intense.

Although there have been many Prada perfumes since the long-awaited first introduction, some of which have been limited editions, overall the Prada Parfums for men and women fall into two categories: the Amber fragrances and the Infusions. Combining exotic notes and essential oils, the Amber range reformulates classic ingredients used in ancient perfumery to create new, modern scents. Presented in oversize, generously thick glass bottles, the Infusions take inspiration from flowers, employing traditional techniques to distill and capture their essence in a meticulous, slow and old-fashioned process. Part of this collection are Infusion d'Iris (a light, fresh scent that evokes memories of Italy, with ingredients such as iris, orange blossom and cedar), Infusion de Fleur d'Oranger and Infusion du Tubéreuse – all creations of leading nose Daniela Andrier.

Right Prada's first women's fragrance was launched in 2004 and came in this classic rectangular glass bottle with the lid to one side. This elegant style of container has since been used for several other Prada fragrances.

Left Prada's first men's fragrance, launched in 2006. A later addition, Infusion D'Homme (seen here) was launched in 2008. It uses the finest artisan traditions of classic perfumery to create a fresh, sensual scent.

Overleaf Prada Candy, launched in 2011, is the latest women's scent to join the Prada perfume family. Designed by perfumer Daniela Andrier, its intense, sweet, exotic scent contains notes of vanilla, caramel and white musk. French actress and model Léa Seydoux, seen here, fronts the ad campaign.

The latest addition to the Prada fragrances – also by Andrier – is Prada Candy, an eau de parfum that is sensual, intense and luxurious in a way that has become synonymous with the range. This particularly sweet scent contains notes of vanilla, caramel and white musk, and is brought to life in a fun campaign starring a beautiful young student (played by French actress Léa Seydoux), who tries to seduce her piano teacher by dancing with him spontaneously. Like the scent, the theatrical number (based on the 1930s Parisian Apache dance) is extremely passionate and dynamic. And the packaging, which merges vibrant Pop influences with classic Art Nouveau, is yet another example of the running thread of Prada's philosophy.

Prada Parfums draws on the brand's heritage in employing traditional methods and focusing on high-quality ingredients, with the attention to detail and expertise only years of hard work and passion can bring. The result is a luxury scent – modern, innovative and different – that, above all, reflects quality with an aura of glamour.

Art & Design

One might say Miuccia Prada's attitude to fashion and her way of using clothes as a form of expression makes her an artist, but the relationship between art and fashion doesn't end there. The name Prada has also come to stand for a strong involvement in, and promotion of, contemporary and avant-garde art. That interest is also seen in the meticulous attention Prada pays to designing their shopping environments.

Following their passion for art, Miuccia Prada and Patrizio Bertelli set up a non-profit foundation called Prada Milano Arte in 1993. It was located in Via Spartaco 8, an old industrial building that would provide a space for exhibitions of exciting contemporary sculpture. The first artists to show were Eliseo Mattiacci, Nino Franchina and David Smith. In 1995, curator and art critic Germano Celant joined the team, and the Foundation was restructured and renamed Fondazione Prada. Its cultural menu expanded to include projects involving photography, art, cinema, design and architecture. The first shows to be sponsored by the new foundation featured the works of Anish Kapoor, Michael Heizer, Louise Bourgeois, Dan Flavin and Walter De Maria. Over time, the foundation has supported a wealth of diverse artists, from Marc Quinn and Sam Taylor-Wood to actor Steve McQueen. With astonishing energy, it has developed and grown, hosting major exhibitions and projects of contemporary art.

In 2008, Prada and Bertelli commissioned the OMA – the think tank of the Office for Metropolitan Architecture – to create a permanent "home" for their art in an early industrial site south of Milan, that included buildings that dated back to 1910. Unveiled in 2015, the headquarters designed by architect Reem Koolhaas are yet another living

Opposite A Prada store art installation, situated at the side of deserted Route 90 in Marfa, Texas. A permanent sculpture by the artists Michael Elmgreen and Ingar Dragset, it was designed to slowly decompose into a natural landscape. Sadly, three days after the sculpture was completed, vandals graffitied the exterior, and broke into the building stealing handbags and shoes.

example of the Prada ethos of fusing old and new in perfect harmony. Modern and, no doubt, ground-breaking constructions, including a 10-storey museum tower, coexist with seven existing restored structures, among them laboratories, brewing silos, warehouses and a large courtyard. This new space is used as a complex to accommodate a series of diverse disciplines ranging from cinema and philosophy to design, fashion and performance art. It also houses works from the permanent collection as well as Prada's archives and those of its Luna Rossa team.

In May 2011, the Fondazione found a new space to showcase its art, this time in Venice's Ca' Corner della Regina – a magnificent baroque palazzo on the Grand Canal, built in 1724 by architect Domenico Rossi. At the time of writing, the palace is being restored by the Fondazione and features a semipermanent exhibition of works from its collection, including pieces by Anish Kapoor, Damien Hirst and Louise Bourgeois.

Right and below A panoramic view of the Fondazione Prada, showcasing modern design in architecture and furniture. The resin sponge wall (right) is one of the features of the Los Angeles Epicenter.

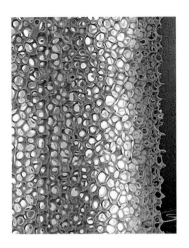

Below In a series of photographic works, Andreas Gursky explores the relationship between art and high consumer culture. Here, the *Prada I*, 1996 depicts the aspirational interior of a Prada Green store with it's pale pink floor, muted green walls and meticulously precise minimal display.

Andreas Gursky, *Prada I*, 1996.
127 x 220 x 6,2 cm.

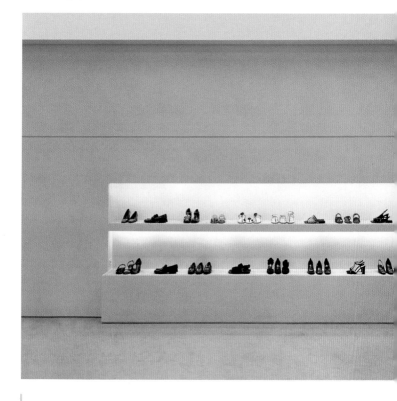

Although it is important to note that fashion and art are kept very separate in the Prada empire, there is of course a strong common denominator to connect them, creating an almost symbiotic relationship: Miuccia Prada herself. Inevitably, both areas reference each other as well as outside influences. The results are often visible on the catwalk. Sometimes they are literal, other times presented with a touch of irony, but always part of an ongoing search: challenging, exploring and deconstructing our preconceptions of beauty. Prada's unusual – even "ugly" at times – colour combinations, interesting textures used out of context, uncomfortable or unusual themes, are all elements that provoke a reaction and make us consider our aesthetic "comfort zone".

Below An art installation by French-American sculptor and artist Louise Bourgeois. *Cell (Clothes)* was a walk-in installation, the size of a small room, that was exhibited in Prada's Ca' Corner della Regina. Bourgeois was one of the first artists to be exhibited by the Fondazione Prada.

Louise Bourgeois, CELL (CLOTHES), 1996.
Wood, glass, fabric, rubber and mixed media,
210.8 x 441.9 x 365.7 cm. Photo: Attilio Maranzano

Art in the Shopping Experience

The foundation also originated the concept and construction of the Prada Epicenters, a series of extraordinary buildings that transcended the traditional use of a store and doubled up as exhibition spaces. From the beginning, the shopping experience has been carefully explored by Prada, their retail venues forming a seamless extension of the brand's philosophy. Despite its global expansion, the company remains unique in its approach to the retail experience. All of its stores offer a luxurious and exclusive environment, together with a level of personal customer service that echoes the intimacy of the original Fratelli Prada shop. In a quest to avoid global homogenization, and in keeping with their philosophy, Prada has developed two types of store: the more conventional "Green Stores" – characterized by iconic pale green walls and simple décor – and the Prada Epicenters, which are conceptual in their architecture, technology and use of space. Each new Epicenter presents an opportunity to break with any preconceptions that might dilute the label's innovative spirit through repetition.

The Prada Epicenters, described by architect Rem Koolhaas of the OMA partnership as "conceptual windows", surpass the traditional shopping experience, merging unconventionally with artistic events such as exhibitions, concerts and film screenings. In 2001 Koolhaas designed the first Epicenter store in Soho, New York. Previously part of the Guggenheim Museum, the building explores the spatial relationship between customer and product to offer new ways of shopping. The way the space is used is reminiscent of a contemporary art gallery, with interactive, changeable features such as its northern wall that connects Broadway and Mercer Street, which becomes a regularly updated mural of Prada wallpaper. Among the groundbreaking technology in this store are glass doors in the changing rooms that become opaque at the touch of a button, "magic mirrors", allowing customers to view themselves moving in slow motion from all angles and a state-of-the-art wireless device enabling staff to access customer data and vast amounts of product information, including sketches and catwalk video-clips. These can instantly be projected for the customer to view on one of the many in-store screens.

Above The first Prada Epicenter, which opened in New York in 2001. The space, the former Soho branch of the Guggenheim Museum, takes up an entire block and includes unique features such as "the wave" staircase, a concave shape that runs the length of the store, and a long wall covered in specially designed wallpaper.

Overleaf Prada Epicenters surpass the shopping experience and become spaces for multifaceted art expression, such as these female silhouettes featured in the New York Epicenter in 2008.

Above Prada's "Fashion's Night Out" theatrical display that took place on 5 November 2011 outside the Tokyo Epicenter. The mannequins wore clothes from the autumn/winter 2011 collection.

Opposite Swiss architects Herzog & de Meuron built Prada's Tokyo Epicenter, located in the Aoyama district, in 2003. Glass panels create a futuristic, yet organic-looking, building.

Built in 2003 by the Swiss architects Herzog & de Meuron, Prada's Tokyo Epicenter is set in the Aoyama district. This six-storey glass building, now iconic for its modern, organic and futuristic design, is made up of diamond-shaped glass panes that create an optical illusion of movement as one walks through the store, with its freestanding floor racks and fibreglass display tables. The building is at its most impressive at night, when illuminated.

In 2004, the Prada Tokyo Epicenter hosted one of the Fondazione's best-known exhibits, "Waist Down" – an exhibition of Miuccia Prada skirts from 1988 to the present day. Skirts have featured in Prada's collections season after season: this show is a rich and colourful visual synopsis, where some skirts are displayed spinning and others swishing. It's a retrospective of the art of haute couture in a journey that displays Miuccia's expression throughout, encapsulating her spirit and creative energy.

"Waist Down" moved to the New York and Los Angeles Epicenters in 2006 and 2009, and from there to Seoul – to the new Prada Transformer, a contemporary structure specifically designed for the exhibition, that was built in the grounds of the sixteenth-century Gyeonghuigung Palace (the Palace of Serene Harmony).

A third Prada Epicenter, built by OMA on Rodeo Drive, Los Angeles in 2004, is characterized by a single slab of aluminium above a minimalist entrance with no traditional shop front. The three-storey venue displays some of its merchandise in large underground cones and has an open ceiling with a skylight. Some features, such as the changing wallpaper displays, link it to the New York Epicenter, while a black-and-white marble floor refers back to the original Fratelli Prada Milan shop.

Above The "Waist Down" exhibition, after it had moved to the Los Angeles Epicenter in 2006. The individual skirts were displayed on metal frames.

Opposite top In another image from LA "Waist Down" exhibition, the cutouts of the model's outfits form a dramatic display in the store.

Opposite below A patterned skirt from the spring/summer 2004 collection on show, encased individually on a flat surface, as part of the "Waist Down" exhibition in Beverly Hills.

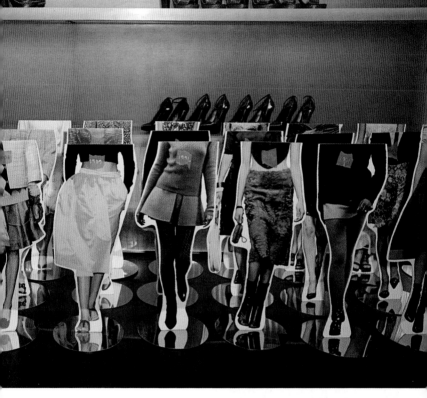

Overleaf As always with Prada, the soul of the brand is echoed throughout. In the Beverly Hills Epicenter, elements of the original Fratelli Prada store in Milan – a black and white tiled marble floor and a selection of luggage – are present, reinforcing the company's strong heritage.

Resources

Further Reading

Angeletti, Norberto, and Oliva, Alberto, *In Vogue : The Illustrated History of the World's Most Famous Fashion Magazine,* Rizzoli, 2006

Baudot, François, *A Century of Fashion,* Thames and Hudson, 1999

Ewing, Elizabeth, *History of Twentieth Century Fashion,* Batsford, 2001

Fogg, Marnie, *The Fashion Design Directory: An A–Z of the Worlds Most Influential Designers and Labels,* Thames and Hudson, 2011

McDowell, Colin, *Fashion Today,* Phaidon, 2000

Mendes, Valerie, and de la Haye, Amy, *20th Century Fashion,* Thames and Hudson, 1999

O'Hara Callan, Georgina, *The Thames and Hudson Dictionary of Fashion and Fashion Designers,* Thames and Hudson, 1998

Polan, Brenda, and Tredre, Roger, *The Great Fashion Designers,* Berg, 2009

Prada, Miuccia, and Bertelli, Patrizio, *Prada,* Progetto Prada Arte, 2009

Collections

Due to the fragility and sensitivity to light, many collections are rotating or on view through special exhibition only. Please see the websites for further information.

The Metropolitan Museum of Art
The Costume Institute
1000 Fifth Avenue
New York, New York 10028-0198, USA
www.metmuseum.org
The Victoria & Albert Museum
Fashion: Level 1
Cromwell Road
London SW7 2RL, UK
www.vam.ac.uk

Prada Exhibition Spaces

Fondazione Prada
Via Fogazarro 36
20135 Milan, Italy

Fondazione Prada (Venice)
Ca Corner della Regina, Santa Croce 2215
30135 Venice, Italy
www.fondazioneprada.org

Prada Transformer
Gyeonghuigung Palace Garden
1-126 Sinmunno 2ga
Jongno-gu, Seoul, Korea
www.prada-transformer.com

Prada Epicenters

Prada Epicenter Broadway
575 Broadway, New York, NY 10012 USA

Prada Post Street
201 Post Street, San Francisco, CA 94108 USA

Prada Epicenter Rodeo Drive
343 North Rodeo Drive, Beverly Hills, Los Angeles, CA 90210 USA

Prada Aoyama
Minato-Ku, Tokyo 107-0062, Japan

Prada
Casa 1/B La Passeggiata, 07020 Porto Cervo, Italy

Index

Page numbers in *italic* refer to illustration captions. Abbreviations S/S and A/W refer to spring/summer and autumn/winter collections.

Acknowledgements

Picture Credits

The publishers would like to thank the following sources for their kind permission to reproduce the pictures in this book.

Key: t=Top, b=Bottom, c=Centre, l=Left and r=Right

Alamy Images: /Prisma Bildagentur AG: 140-141
© Louise Bourgeois Trust: /DACS, London /VAGA, New York 2011: 144
Camera Press: 50, 58, 71, /Anthea Simms: 23, /Andreas Them: 24, 51, 97r
© Carlton Books: 20tr, 20cr, 20bl
Catwalking: 1, 2, 3, 4, 6, 26, 28, 29, 30, 31, 37, 38, 39, 40l, 40r, 41, 42, 44, 43, 52l, 52r, 54, 55, 56, 57, 59, 60, 61, 63, 64, 65, 66l, 66r, 68, 69 (Main & Inset), 70, 74, 75, 77l, 77r, 80, 81, 82, 83, 84, 85, 86, 87, 89, 89, 90, 91, 92l, 92r, 97l, 98, 99, 100, 102, 103, 106, 107l, 107r, 108, 109, 111, 112, 113, 114, 115l, 115r, 116, 118, 119, 122, 124l, 124r, 125, 127l, 128
Corbis: /Michel Arnaud /Beateworks: 138, /Condé Nast Archive: 12, /Julio Donoso/Sygma: 32, 33, / © Liz Hafalia/San Francisco Chronicle: 78, /WWD/Condé Nast: 48, 73, 76, 121b
Courtesy Gallery Sprueth/Magers: /© DACS, London 2011: 142-143
Getty Images: 18-19, 21, 22, 136-137, 152, 153t, 153b, 154-155, /AFP: 72, 104, 105, 123l, 123r, /Cover: 15, /Gamma-Rapho: 127r, 146-147, /James Leynse: 151, /Time & Life Pictures: 133l, / WireImage: 46-47, 121t, 150
Kerry Taylor Auctions: 34, 35
Patrice de Villiers: 132
Picture Desk: /The Art Archive /Kharbine-Tapabor /© ADAGP, Paris and DACS, London 2011.: 120
Pixelformula/SIPA/REX/Shutterstock: 130r, 131
Private Collection: 43, 101t, 101b
Rex Features: /Corri Corrado: 88, /Tobi Jenkins /Daily Mail: 133r, 134, 135, /Veronique Louis: 148-149, /Caroline Mardon: 13, /Olycom SPA: 94
Topfoto.co.uk: /Alinari: 10-11, /Caro /Teschner: 8, 25
Victor Virgile/Gamma-Rapho via Getty Images: 130l

Author Acknowledgements

I would like to thank everyone who has supported me throughout the making of this book – especially fashion designers Chris Mossom and Holger Auffenberg for sharing their insight with me, Lucia Graves, Natalia Farran and Russell Woollen for their input, and editor Lisa Dyer for her invaluable direction.

LITTLE BOOK OF

Gucci

Published in 2020 by Welbeck
An Imprint of HEADLINE PUBLISHING GROUP

35

Design and layout © Carlton Books Limited 2020
Text © Karen Homer 2020

Cataloguing in Publication Data is available from the British Library

ISBN 978-1-78739-458-2

Printed in China

HEADLINE PUBLISHING GROUP
An Hachette UK Company, Carmelite House
50 Victoria Embankment, London EC4Y 0DZ

www.headline.co.uk
www.hachette.co.uk

LITTLE BOOK OF

Gucci

The story of the iconic fashion house

KAREN HOMER

WELBECK

Contents

INTRODUCTION

Gucci

A versatile slang term based on the luxury fashion brand meaning okay/good/great/awesome/fresh/etc. Originally used in the streets but now popularized by the masses ... To be "all Gucci" is a wonderful thing indeed.

– Urban Dictionary

In 2021 Gucci will celebrate the 100th anniversary of Guccio Gucci opening his long-dreamed-of eponymous luxury leather goods store in Florence. In the past century the company has overcome many challenges, yet has managed to reinvent itself on several occasions and not only survive but thrive.

During the Second World War the problems were of a practical nature, with shortages of leather forcing other companies to close. Gucci, however, looked elsewhere and his resourceful solution - printing hemp fabric with the house pattern – not only enabled the business to continue producing luggage but also created an iconic design. After Guccio's death in 1953, the company passed into the hands of his sons Aldo, Rodolfo and Vasco and initially blossomed, with new designs, celebrity endorsements, high sales and global expansion. By the 1970s and 1980s, however, as Gucci's grandsons took a greater hand in the firm, more complicated issues arose, with family in-fighting leading to acrimonious legal challenges and a company on the verge of bankruptcy.

OPPOSITE In the Gucci Resort 2019 show, Alessandro Michele showed his veneration for the signature Gucci Diamante pattern but gave it his own twist.

RIGHT In the 1960s,
Gucci expanded their
offerings to included
fragrance lines
for both men and
women, a relatively
inexpensive way to
buy into the status of
the brand.

The 1990s were make or break for Gucci, now owned by
investment bank Investcorp, and the failing label employed a
young, unknown designer, Tom Ford, in part because no one
else would take the job. Alongside new CEO Domenico De
Sole, Ford turned the company's fortunes around, reinventing
the somewhat staid, traditional label with a massive injection
of sex appeal and glamour, to make the double-G logo one of
the most coveted status symbols of that hedonistic decade. Ford
stayed until 2004, when, among rumours of a falling-out with
Gucci's parent company, he left to start his own label.

The creative directorship of Gucci during the following
decade was held by Italian designer Frida Giannini. Although
her stewardship of the label has been criticized by some as too
traditional and unimaginative, her cool, calm and collected
demeanour, along with a native understanding of Gucci's
customer base, allowed the brand to hold steady in a difficult
economic climate. And to give credit where it's due, Giannini

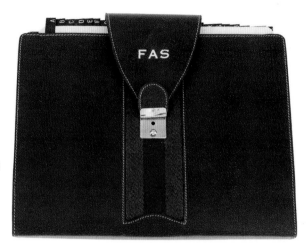

RIGHT This monogrammed Gucci address book belonging to Frank Sinatra shows how ubiquitous the brand has been in the lives of twentieth century cultural icons.

designed a number of signature pieces that would become modern classics.

By 2014, the brand was slipping once again. This was in part due to the changing landscape of fashion since the millennium. As well as the influence of the Internet and social media, which radically altered the way fashion reached consumers, a kind of reverse snobbery had seen designer labels fall out of favour as aspirational status symbols. Luxury brands were forced to reinvent themselves, and, for Gucci, that transformation came at the hands of another relative unknown: Alessandro Michele.

Michele, with his "eclectic and flamboyant aesthetic" (*The Telegraph*) has been designer-in-chief at Gucci since 2015 and is probably the most exciting fashion designer of our times. His eccentric genius is lauded not only by fashion pundits but also by millennial style commentators and, of course, shoppers themselves. His talent at combining historical influences with streetwear, the gender fluidity of his garments and show casting,

RIGHT Kendall Jenner wearing the signature Marmont belt, the most wanted product of 2018 on Lyst.

and the sheer technical skill of the design team, have allowed the label to reach the very pinnacle of fashion, fame and fortune.

Guccio Gucci's original dream was to make fine leather luggage for the social elite. A century later, the Gucci signature print or double-G logo is as likely to be seen on the bum bag or fanny pack of a hip-hop star or the belt of an off-duty model – the new social elite – as on the traditional handbag of a Euro royal. Unimaginable as it might have seemed to Gucci and his sons, their label is no longer just for aristocrats and social climbers – it is now for the Instagram generation.

RIGHT Rapper Gucci Mane arrives at the Spring/Summer 2020 show in Milan.

The Early
Years

BEGINNINGS
OF AN ICONIC BRAND

Guccio Gucci was born on 28 March, 1881, in the Tuscan
city of Florence. His father was a modestly successful
leather craftsman and milliner who came from a long line
of leather-makers.

However – ironically, given his future success – the young
Gucci rejected the family trade, preferring instead to
leave Italy to travel and work in Europe. In his late teens
he arrived first in Paris, then settled for several years in London,
where he worked at The Savoy hotel, starting as a busboy and
rising to the respected position of maître d'.

During his time working at The Savoy, Gucci dealt with the
many glamorous celebrities and royals of the day who stayed in
the hotel, and he observed in particular that they always travelled
with volumes of beautifully crafted, refined luggage. He also
became fascinated by London's many traditional craftsmen and
leather-makers, especially the company H.J. Cave & Sons, which
supplied the highest quality goods to those wealthy enough to
afford them. Lastly, Gucci noticed that many of these aristocrats
had an obsession with polo playing and horse racing, something
that would influence his designs from the very beginning.

OPPOSITE Guccio Gucci, the patriarch of the Gucci family business.
It was his dream from when he was a teenage porter at London's
Savoy hotel to found his own luxury leather goods label.

RIGHT The glamorous Savoy hotel in London played host to some of the biggest names and celebrities of the day. Working as a busboy, Guccio Gucci was inspired by the style and refinement of its guests.

On his return to Italy, just after the turn of the twentieth century, Gucci joined the Milan leather manufacturer Franzi (Gucci's father's business having gone bankrupt), and there he learned the trade that would eventually make him a household name. Over the next decade he worked diligently for Franzi, while dreaming of his own business. He slowly began to design and produce leather goods, culminating in a move back to Florence in 1920 and the opening of his first eponymous store on Via della Vigna Nuova in 1921.

Harking back to his years observing the wealthy guests at London's Savoy hotel, and wanting to target this social class with his luxury goods, Gucci's earliest leather creations were saddles and saddlebags. Despite the fact that demand for these goods was beginning to fall at the beginning of the twentieth century, thanks to the rise in automobiles, Gucci never lost his taste for equestrian style, and riding-inspired embellishments

RIGHT From circa 1900, this photochromic image shows Guccio Gucci's beloved hometown of Florence. Gucci finally opened his eponymous store on Via della Vigna Nuova in 1921.

became a big part of the brand's heritage, and they continue to be used by the label to this day.

Having so admired the traditional leather-makers in London, from the very beginning of his business Gucci emphasized using the most accomplished Tuscan artisans and, alongside his store, founded a workshop so that he had complete control over the quality of the leather goods he supplied. In fact, Gucci was so devoted to the British tradition of craftsmanship that advertisements from the time promote the store as stocking "English leather goods". Gucci was also unusually aware of the changing status of women, who were becoming increasingly emancipated during the 1920s. In a 1924 letter Gucci wrote about his new range of "ladies' bags", which would become a huge part of Gucci's product line in later years.

As the demand for equestrian goods waned, he began supplying pieces of luggage, and within a decade handbags, gloves, shoes and belts had been added to his repertoire. During the 1920s and early 1930s, Gucci's reputation grew ever stronger and the wealthy flocked to Florence not only for saddlery but for the label's other high-quality leather products.

In 1901 Gucci married Aida Calvelli, a seamstress, and the couple raised six children: a daughter, Grimalda; and four sons,

Enzo (who tragically died aged nine), Aldo, Vasco, Rodolfo (who gained fame as a movie actor under the stage name Maurizio D'Ancora before joining the family firm) and Ugo, Aida's son whom Guccio adopted. Gucci's sons Aldo, Rodolfo, Vasco and Ugo would all become involved in the company, both on the design and business sides.

Aldo, the first of the sons to join the company, in 1933, would become one of the greatest influences on the success of the family firm. He was an extremely talented designer and also a savvy businessman, and under his guidance during the 1930s the Gucci brand and its logos became firmly established. Aldo immediately saw the need for an official emblem to make

RIGHT Guccio Gucci and his wife in Italy in the late 1940s, enjoying the success of his business. Aida carries a fine leather bag that epitomizes Gucci quality.

Gucci's products stand out, and in a stroke of genius he took the double Gs from his father's name and designed the interlocking pattern that is so instantly recognizable today. As a brand logo it is an immensely clever, simple, yet aesthetic design. The fact that it is not immediately obvious that it is made up of two letter Gs (so is usually shown beneath the name Gucci itself) has helped create an aspirational logo that is still in use almost 90 years later. Over the years it has been used diversely across the Gucci range: printed onto every conceivable fabric for clothes, embossed onto leather accessories, forged into metal clasps for bags and belts, made into hosiery and been transformed into interlinking bracelets, watch straps and rings.

RIGHT An example of the interlocking GG Diamante that Aldo designed in the 1930s at that is still universally recognized to this day.

RIGHT Maurizio, son of Rodolfo, took over as the head of the fashion house in the 1980s, selling the company and his grandfather's legacy in 1993.

As the beginning of the Second World War approached, Italy fell under Mussolini's fascism, and, as a result of the country's alliance with Nazi Germany, the League of Nations imposed sanctions that severely limited the import of leather. Forced to find an alternative, Guccio experimented with jute and linen, eventually settling on a specially woven, plain hemp fabric from Naples. Onto this he printed the company's first signature pattern: a series of small, interconnecting diamonds in dark brown on a tan background, an early version of what became known as the "Diamante" print. The patterned fabric, created to distinguish the Gucci brand from competitors, was made into some of the first Gucci suitcases and trunks, and proved hugely successful.

The material shortages during and after the war led Guccio to create another unlikely component that became part of a signature piece in the brand's history, and that is still produced today: the burnished semi-circular cane handle for his Bamboo bag, the body of which was originally shaped like a horse's saddle. The creation of these two substitutes – the bamboo handle and the printed hemp cloth – illustrated the Gucci family's resourcefulness and determination to succeed, and, where other companies closed down, the Gucci brand continued to grow. While the company resumed the use of leather when it was once more freely available, adopting pigskin as its house material, the immediately recognizable printed fabric remained. Guccio's wartime inventions proved to be some of the label's most iconic products.

Before the war, Gucci had opened one other store, on Rome's Via Condotti in 1938. This was followed in 1951 by a flagship opening on the elite Via Monte Napoleone in Milan, part of the fashion district and reputed to be Europe's most expensive street. Two years later, in 1953, Aldo oversaw the opening of the brand's first store in the United States, in New York's Savoy-Plaza Hotel – recalling Guccio's dreams from his time working at London's legendary Savoy hotel – but just two weeks later, Guccio died in Milan, aged 72. The family was in turmoil, especially when ugly facts surfaced about who was to take over the company: Gucci's daughter Grimalda – who had long been employed in the family firm – had not been left any share in the company. The same was true of Guccio's adopted son Ugo; he had already lost his stake through a troubled relationship with Guccio, who protested Ugo's membership of the National Fascist Party. In the end it was left to the three brothers, Aldo, Rodolfo and Vasco to honour their father's legacy and to continue to take the House of Gucci from strength to strength, into the future.

Signature
Pieces

PRICELESS LUXURY

"Quality is remembered long after the price is forgotten."

– Aldo Gucci

The death of Guccio Gucci in 1953, just two weeks after his first New York store opened, saw the firm pass into the control of his sons Aldo and Rodolfo (with Vasco and Ugo playing smaller parts in the business). The brothers were determined to keep their father's dream of an elite brand alive, and continued to focus on creating only the most memorable fine leather goods and accessories, which increasingly became coveted by the rich and famous. Aldo, in particular, had already proved his flair for both design and business, creating the iconic interlocking GG logo in the 1930s and helping to create the signature Diamante-printed fabric for luggage, which was a precursor to the Gucci trunks and bags so recognizable today.

In 1953 Aldo created possibly the most iconic of all of Gucci's products: the Horsebit loafer. Although his father had produced fine leather shoes with metal snaffles as early as 1932, Aldo redesigned the loafer and, in homage to his father's love of equestrian embellishments, added a gilded metal snaffle in

OPPOSITE Grace Kelly wearing the Flora silk scarf commissioned for her by Rodolfo Gucci and designed by Italian illustrator Vittorio Accornero in 1966. The print went on to be one of Gucci's most iconic patterns.

RIGHT An image of Dirk Bogarde wearing Gucci's Horsebit loafer in 1960. Designed by Aldo in 1953 in homage to his father's love of all things equestrian, it has a gilded metal snaffle in the shape of a horse's bit.

the shape of the mouthpiece on a horse's bridle. An immediate success, the simple yet elegant Gucci loafer has become one of the fashion world's most coveted status symbols – so important in fashion history that since 1985 it has been on permanent display at New York's Metropolitan Museum of Art.

The Horsebit motif itself subsequently became a detail that was added to many different accessories in many different ways. As a metal fastening it formed clasps for bags and belts, and much later was adorned with sequins by Frida Giannini, who created jewellery and chain-link straps out of the pattern. During the 1960s the Horsebit began to be printed onto fabric including silk and wool ties, scarves and clothing, and in the 1970s use of the print intensified further, with it appearing even on homewares that Gucci had started to offer. With Tom Ford's dramatic revival of the Gucci label in the 1990s, the Horsebit was given an ultra-stylized edge, appearing on high-heeled, patent red loafers and as oversized fastenings on belts and bags.

RIGHT The Gucci loafer has become so much a part of fashion history that it has been on permanent display at New York's Metropolitan Museum since 1985.

RIGHT The Horsebit motif was worked into many different forms including elegant gold chainlink jewellery.

Another equestrian-inspired creation that has become synonymous with the Gucci brand is the striped green–red–green grosgrain web fabric, inspired by the girth that circles a horse's body to hold the saddle on its back. The colours are said to have been chosen for their resemblance to traditional British fox-hunting jackets, and the stripe brings to mind military medal ribbons or public school scarves, both carrying connotations of aristocratic status. Over the years this signature woven fabric has been made into every conceivable product including belts, bag straps, scarves, watch straps and thongs for flip-flops, and has adorned everything from clothing to trainers. While Gucci has experimented with various different colours, most often with blue replacing the central red of the striped band, it is this red–green combination that remains most iconic, an instant identifier of the Gucci brand.

In the same year as Aldo designed the Horsebit loafer, he also reworked the Diamante fabric print, incorporating the double-G logo into the centre of the interconnecting diamonds, but keeping the same colours of dark brown on a tan background. This GG print, as it has become known, is crafted out of hard-wearing cotton canvas fabric, finished with a leather trim and often combined, in handbags and other small accessories, with the woven green–red–green web stripe. Again, the signature print has appeared on many different accessories, including wallets, shoes and hats, as well as being printed onto finer fabric to make clothing. In 1955 Aldo finally trademarked the interlocking Gs logo, it having become a sought-after status symbol, and it was subsequently routinely added to all Gucci products.

Accessories were very much the core of the Gucci brand during the 1950s and 1960s, and one handbag in particular became another signature piece that is still produced today: the Bamboo bag. Originally designed by Guccio, the saddle-shaped

OPPOSITE Charlotte Casiraghi models the Gucci signature Horsebit loafer, its metal snaffle based on a horse's mouthpiece, in 2017. The quintessentially stylish royal equestrian and granddaughter to Grace Kelly could not be a more fitting ambassador for the heritage range.

FOREVER NOW

Icons of Heritage: the Horsebit.
Equestrian signature of the Gucci loafer.

RIGHT Gucci's signature pattern, the double-G printed canvas fabric, was designed in 1953 by Aldo Gucci, a reworking of the original hemp Diamante print created by Guccio Gucci during the Second World War when the embargo on importing leather into Italy forced him to find new materials to work with.

bag is carried by a burnished bamboo-cane handle created out of necessity during the wartime leather embargo. Its covetable status increased as Hollywood legends including Ingrid Bergman and Elizabeth Taylor were spotted carrying it, and in later years it was a firm favourite of Princess Diana.

Renaming an accessory after a celebrity has created some of the most iconic bags of the twentieth century, and one of these is the Gucci "Jackie", dedicated to Jackie Kennedy, who in 1961, at the height of her popularity as the most stylish woman in the world, was photographed carrying an unstructured, unisex Gucci tote. It sparked a frenzy of copycat purchases and the Jackie became an integral part of the brand's collections during the 1960s. It was subsequently resurrected from the archives in the 1990s under Ford, and again in 2009 under Giannini, who renamed it "New Jackie", thus sealing its reputation as one of the most famous it-bags of all time. Another First Lady who was associated with

RIGHT The signature double-G printed fabric has been reworked in many different colours including classic red as shown in this small train case and black with a striking black-red web stripe in this version of the original GG Boston bag.

impeccable taste and style – and who also was devoted to Gucci – was Nancy Reagan. Legend has it that comedian Bob Hope, a family friend of the Reagans, teased Nancy that her personal nurse would tickle her under the chin with the words "Gucci, Gucci, goo!"

The patronage of celebrities was heavily encouraged by the Gucci family, who realized what the connection between their brand and glamorous socialites and actresses was worth. When, in 1966, Grace Kelly visited the atelier to buy a bamboo-handled bag, Rodolfo Gucci wanted to give the stylish princess a gift, but after deeming nothing in the label's collection suitable, he commissioned Italian illustrator Vittorio Accornero to design a painterly floral scarf in her honour. The print Accornero created – which featured 43 types of flowers, plants and insects in a vibrant kaleidoscope of 37 colours – was labelled the "Flora" and became a signature of the Gucci brand. Forever associated with the glamorous Hollywood-actress-turned-Princess-of-Monaco, it was an immediate success and inspired decades of floral designs among Gucci's silk accessories, including a relaunch of the pattern on canvas bags by designer Giannini in 2005.

The Gucci brand's long association with celebrities in film and music also helped the brand establish itself as the maker of iconic pieces. In the late 1940s and early 1950s, Gucci's bags appeared in Ingrid Bergman films – she carries a wooden-handled bag in Roberto Rossellini's *Stromboli*, a structured leather bag in *Europa '51* and a Bamboo bag in *Viaggio in Italia*. A friendship between the fashion label and filmmaker Michelangelo Antonioni led to Gucci bags appearing in films throughout the 1950s and early 1960s. Other actors were also drawn to the glamour of Gucci's products, and the company's historical archives feature images of many recognizable faces, including Audrey Hepburn, Peter Sellers, Sophia Loren and Elizabeth Taylor, visiting Gucci stores.

OPPOSITE Jackie Kennedy Onassis made the slouchy Gucci hobo bag an instant classic when she was photographed in 1961, reputedly using the handbag to shield herself from the paparazzi. She was subsequently regularly spotted carrying a version of the label's signature accessory which was renamed the "Jackie" in her honour.

LEFT Grace Kelly leaving Gucci's flagship Rome store in 1959. The endorsement of royalty and celebrities like the Princess of Monaco greatly increased the reputation of the fashion label.

LEFT Audrey Hepburn with her husband, Mel Ferrer, and son in 1964. The actress and style icon carries a patent Gucci handbag with chain strap.

RIGHT A detailed shot of the Gucci signature Flora pattern, which features 43 types of flowers, plants and insects in a vibrant kaleidoscope using 37 colours.

In later years, too, the brand's instantly recognizable monogrammed fabric, striped belts and Horsebit loafers appeared in numerous Bond films, instantly imparting a sophisticated Euro-glamour, perfectly suited to the filmic world of international espionage. Similarly, later films including *Pretty Woman* and *Wall Street* have cameo appearances by Gucci storefronts and glamorous products, showing quite how strongly associated the brand is with wealth, status and conspicuous consumption.

By the end of the 1960s, Gucci's success in establishing its monogrammed Diamante fabric, interlocking Gs motif and red-and-green stripe contributed to the brand's global recognition as an aspirational fashion label, competing with the likes of Chanel and Louis Vuitton. But, despite the reputation of the brand, there were challenges ahead, as Gucci sought to expand over the next few decades.

LEFT By the 1950s Gucci had become one of the most high-end accessories brands. In this *Vogue* shot from 1956 the model carries a classic bamboo-handled structured black leather handbag with gold fastening.

OPPOSITE Gucci had a long association with film, with their bags frequently being used on screen, and many actors were fans of the label. Here Peter Sellers walks out of the Gucci boutique in Rome in 1966.

Going Global

NOT COUNTING THE COST

Smooth travellers in the luxury class. Quintet of cases, read to take flight in royal blue canvas, brilliantly strapped in scarle leather, shiningly buckled in gilt. Three perfectly matche cases, stepped up in size. Impeccable hat box; light, flexibl holdall, side-locking. The set costs £114 18s. or the piece can be bought separately. All by Gucci, New Bond St, Londo

Pearls: Jewelcraft. Photograph by Frank Whitchu

AN EXPANDING
EMPIRE

From the 1960s onward, the Gucci heirs were determined
to capitalize on their father Guccio's legacy, and spread the
family firm across the globe.

While Rodolfo and Vasco remained in Milan and
Florence respectively, Aldo continued to run the
operation in the US, where in 1960 the store had
moved from New York's Savoy-Plaza Hotel to a prominent
Fifth Avenue location. Following on from the London and Palm
Beach openings, in 1963 Gucci arrived in Paris, and with Europe
and the United States won over to the glamour of the Gucci
label, Aldo began to look east for future expansion. In 1972 a
store opened in Tokyo, with a larger flagship store opening in
Hong Kong two years later. This was a lucrative period for the
fashion house, as at the same time it was rapidly increasing its
clothing component, opening a standalone boutique in New
York dedicated to Gucci's clothing line.

During the 1970s, Rodolfo's son Maurizio had joined his uncle
Aldo in New York, playing a large part in the running of the

OPPOSITE Since the very beginning Gucci had positioned itself
as a luxury brand. As Aldo famously said: "Quality is remembered
long after the price is forgotten". An advert from the 1960s
illustrates this successful marketing strategy perfectly.

RIGHT Aldo Gucci, shown here at the opening of the London store in 1977, was the eldest of Guccio's sons and was dedicated to the firm his whole life, since joining in 1933. He was hugely instrumental in the global expansion of the brand both as a designer and businessman, opening stores in the United States and Far East.

company. However, with the advent of the new generation of Guccis, the label was soon to become notorious for its familial in-fighting, rather than just famous for its fashion credentials. First, in 1980, Aldo's son, Paolo, left the company to start his own fashion label under the name Paolo Gucci, leaning heavily on the 1966 signature Flora print for inspiration for his collection. Lawsuits were filed forbidding him to use the Gucci name and he was blocked. But in the fallout, Aldo himself was prosecuted in the United States for tax evasion, with Paolo testifying against his father until, eventually, in 1986 Aldo

RIGHT Rodolfo
Gucci, shown here
in 1971 front of the
Milan store where
he was based, was
also a major part
of his father's firm,
but as Aldo and
Rodolfo's sons joined
the company in
the 1970s, family
infighting started to
threaten the brand's
success.

RIGHT Despite the brand's financial struggles, they continued to maintain the facade of success. The Gucci store on New York's Fifth Avenue, shown here in 1985, was one of the most prominent on the fashionable street.

pleaded guilty to non-payment of $7 million of tax money, earning himself a year's imprisonment. Meanwhile the death of Rodolfo in 1983 saw his son Maurizio grasp the leadership of the company for himself, first bringing on board a financial lawyer, Domenico De Sole, as president of Gucci America, and eventually ousting Aldo and his children, forcing them to sell their shares in the company. In retaliation Aldo accused Maurizio of forging his father's signatures on documents that transferred half of the company's shares to him alone. The company was floundering amid gossip and poor management.

RIGHT In 1980 Aldo's son Paolo left the business to start his own fashion label, also called Gucci. His designs drew heavily on the signature 1966 Flora print, which led to legal action being taken by his father to stop him.

Despite showing the label's first ready-to-wear collection to great acclaim at the 1981 Florence fashion shows, Gucci's fortunes continued to wane during the 1980s. Maurizio had none of his father's or uncle's design flair or business acumen, and with the continued mud-slinging from the rejected members of his family, the reputation of the brand took a nosedive. Finally, in 1988, Domenico De Sole persuaded Maurizio to sell a large stake of the Gucci company to Bahrain-based investment bank Investcorp, taking control of Guccio's company out of the family's hands. With new investment, Maurizio brought on board Dawn Mello, an American fashion executive then working at Bergdorf Goodman. Mello immediately advised expanding Gucci's ready-to-wear business, widening the brand from just an accessories label. In order to do so, in 1990 she hired a young designer, Tom Ford.

An immediate success, Ford became Design Director of all products within two years, but internal squabbles still dogged the brand. Maurizio finally liquidated his shares in 1993, with the company on the verge of bankruptcy after constant arguing with his partners about both business and artistic direction. In 1994 Mello left the company to return to Bergdorf Goodman. Ford took over as Creative Director and Guccio's heirs were no longer part of the fashion label that carried their name.

In a dramatic twist worthy of the worst stereotypes about Italian dynastic families, just 18 months after Maurizio divested himself of the last of his shares in the company, he was gunned down in the lobby of his elegant Milan offices. Suspicion fell immediately on his glamorous ex-wife Patrizia Reggiani, who had married Maurizio in 1972 and been catapulted into a life of glamour and celebrity as half of the famed "Gucci couple". With homes in Acapulco, Connecticut and St Moritz, a private yacht, and a luxury penthouse in New York, they fraternized

OPPOSITE The 1980s and 1990s were turbulent decades for the Gucci brand with Maurizio first selling the majority of his shares to investment bank, Investcorp, and finally leaving the company in 1993. Further scandal dogged the brand when Maurizio was gunned down in the lobby of his Milan office. Two years after his death his ex-wife, Patrizia Reggiani, was accused of hiring a hitman to kill him.

with the world's social elite including Jackie Onassis and the Kennedy clan. But Rodolfo's death in 1983, and the subsequent in-fighting and dramatic decline in the fortunes of the business – something Reggiani claims could have been avoided had Maurizio listened to her – damaged the marriage irreparably and the couple divorced. Three years after his death, Reggiani was convicted of hiring a hit man to murder him. In a 2016 interview in the *Guardian*, after her release from prison, she was quoted as saying about their relationship falling apart, "I was angry with Maurizio about ... losing the family business. It was stupid. It was a failure. I was filled with rage, but there was nothing I could do."

Thankfully for the House of Gucci, under the dream team of Tom Ford and Domenico De Sole – or "Dom and Tom" as they became known within the industry – the brand reinvented itself, injecting glamour and sex alongside design expertise and a talent for the business of fashion. In 1995 De Sole made part of the company public, and both the profit and stock value of Gucci quickly rose. The final chapter in the saga of Gucci's ownership came in the late 1990s when first Prada, one of Gucci's direct competitors, then Bernard Arnault, chairman of the luxury goods mega-group LVMH, moved to purchase a controlling portion of Gucci shares. Horrified at losing control, De Sole brought in François-Henri Pinault, chairman of the retail giant PPR (Pinault-Printemps-Redoute), who bought a 40 per cent stake in Gucci. Positioning itself in direct competition with LVMH, the PPR group subsequently bought more designer brands including Yves Saint Laurent, Balenciaga and Bottega Veneta. By the end of the century, Gucci was the flagship name in a global luxury brands empire, with all the resources and power that brought.

OPPOSITE Gucci's association with equestrian sport included sponsoring polo events that were also tied in with the brand's aspirational image. Here Prince Charles holds his Gucci polo prize in Windsor in 1983.

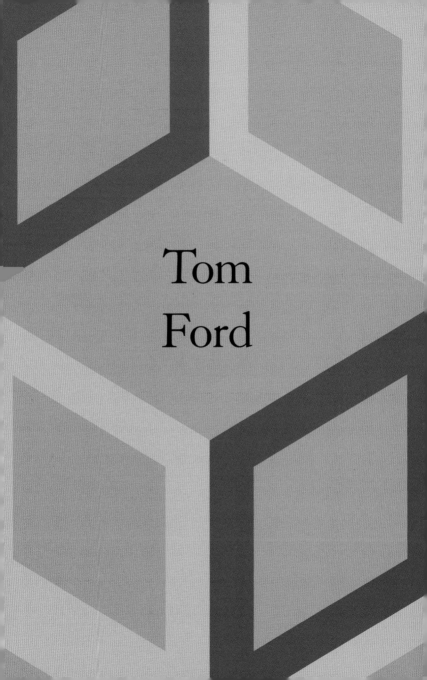

Tom
Ford

A SEXUAL
REVOLUTION

Today Tom Ford is recognized as one of the greatest fashion designers of the past 30 years and is rightly credited with turning around the fortunes of the Gucci label.

A t the time of his appointment to the ailing fashion house by Dawn Mello in 1990, Ford had none of the experience, credentials or reputation one might have expected of a creative director of a major brand.

Born in Austin, Texas, in 1961, the young Tom Ford moved to New York City in 1979 to study history of art at NYU (New York University). However it was the social scene that opened Ford's eyes to both a career within the fashion world and the possibilities the city had to offer. In a later interview with *Vogue* magazine, he remembered being invited to a party: "Andy Warhol was [there], and he took us to Studio 54 – wow. Even today, I still start shaking when I hear Donna Summer because it's the music of my coming of age."

OPPOSITE A young Kate Moss models a sensual, 1970s-inspired outfit from Tom Ford's groundbreaking 1995 catwalk show. The purple satin silk shirt, buttoned low and tucked into hipster trousers with a slim Gucci belt, is topped with a matching velvet jacket and patent, high-heeled Horsebit loafers.

RIGHT Supermodel Amber Valletta wears a silk velvet dress and matching coat as part of Ford's Gucci Autumn/Winter 1995 collection, which inspired a trend for head-to-toe velvet and satin.

Studio 54 became a regular haunt of Ford's, where he mingled with the likes of Halston, Bianca Jagger and Jerry Hall as well as with Warhol himself, and the glamorous, sensual fashion styles of this period formed the foundation of the Ford designs that transformed Gucci's fortunes.

After a year of study, Ford dropped out of NYU to focus on an acting career in LA. His good looks lead to castings in a number of national advertising campaigns, experiences that later helped him reshape the Gucci advertising strategy to great success.

RIGHT Model Kylie
Bax sashays down
the catwalk in the
Autumn/Winter 1996
collection. Her palely
glamorous silk shirt
is unbuttoned to
the waist to reveal
a statement gold
necklace and matching
flowing trousers have
a Halston vibe that
wouldn't have been
out of place on Bianca
Jagger in her Studio
54 days.

These early years as an actor sparked a lifelong passion for filmmaking, which became a second career for the designer in 2005 with the launch of his own production company, Fade to Black.

Returning to New York, Ford enrolled on an architecture course at Parsons School of Design. However, he quickly decided that he would prefer to pursue a career in fashion, selectively editing his resumé when he started to apply for fashion roles, by neglecting to specify the exact subject of his degree. Similarly, a stint in France as an employee of Parisian company Chloé found its way onto his CV, but Ford glossed over the fact that it was in fact a PR company and not the fashion label for whom he had worked. Through his persistence and ability to charm those he met, Ford eventually secured a position as design assistant to American designer Cathy Hardwick, who remembers his interview: "I had every intention of giving him no hope. I asked him who his favourite European designers were. He said, 'Armani and Chanel'. Months later I asked him why he said that and he said, 'Because you were wearing something Armani.' Is it any wonder he got the job?"

Ford worked for Hardwick for two years, until his appointment by Mello in 1990 to head up women's ready-to-wear at Gucci. While this might seem like a massive promotion for the relatively inexperienced young designer, it is important to remember that at the time virtually no one in fashion wanted to work for Gucci, let alone relocate to Milan, a condition of the role. As Mello explained, "I was talking to a lot of people, and most didn't want the job. For an American designer to move to Italy, to join a company that was far from being a brand, would have been pretty risky."

Nevertheless, Ford took the position and moved to Milan with his partner, fashion journalist Richard Buckley, a constant support in his life. (They finally married in 2014, having been in a relationship for three decades.) In 1994, two years after his move to Milan, Ford's role expanded to include overseeing fragrance, advertising and the design of the Gucci stores, and when Mello left the company in 1994 to return to Bergdorf

RIGHT Madonna was such a fan of Ford's breakaway 1995 Autumn/Winter show that she wore one of the collection's most recognizable outfits to that year's MTV awards. The turquoise satin shirt – unbuttoned to reveal the singer's bra – and Horsebit belt instantly sealed the new designer's reputation.

Goodman, Ford became Creative Director, finally stepping into the spotlight. With the unwavering support of President and CEO Domenico De Sole, Ford rapidly stamped his mark on the struggling brand.

The few reviews that Ford's debut collection in 1994 did receive were mixed, with hardly any fashion writers bothering to even watch the show. *Vogue* magazine's Sarah Mower remembers the Gucci publicist pleading with style journalists to attend his debut and yet, just one year later, the fashion crowd flocked to see Ford's groundbreaking Autumn/Winter 1995 collection. After the severity of 1980s power dressing, with its monotone colours and sharply-drawn lines, followed by early 90s shapeless grunge, Ford's louche, overtly sexual designs were an eye-opener. Drawing heavily on his experience at Studio 54 and the luxe-glam of 1970s styles, his designs included fitted satin shirts in jewel-like colours, unbuttoned almost to the waist on both men and women, paired with hip-hugging velvet bell-bottoms, velvet suits in electric orange and lime green, and richly textured coats of vivid blue. It was an assault on the senses, full of hedonistic indulgence in the form of luxurious fur, velvet, leather and satin, worn by models including Amber Valletta and Kate Moss, who sashayed sexily down the catwalk. Ford's collection was so new and bold that it has been widely credited with transforming the landscape of fashion.

Ford had not forgotten Gucci's heritage – the Horsebit loafer was still very much in evidence – but instead of playing it safe with the traditional values of the label, he had taken a brand which was essentially classic and blown it out of the water. A huge hit with the fashion press and high-profile celebrities including Madonna, who wore a key look from the collection to that year's MTV Music Awards, the charismatic Tom Ford had definitely arrived.

OPPOSITE Ford was the first of Gucci's head designers to incorporate an element of androgyny in his designs. Here a half-unbuttoned, fitted pinstriped blouse and matching trousers from his Spring/Summer 1996 show is an ironic nod to the pinstripe suits beloved of Wall Street bankers. Fittingly, costume designer Ellen Mirojnick confirms that she always put the character of Gordon Gekko from the *Wall Street* films in Gucci loafers.

A year later, the designer acknowledged his 1996 Autumn/ Winter show was when "it all came together for the first time". Ford's hyper-sexual designs, harking back to Studio 54 with a risqué Helmut Newton-style influence, shocked the world and was a welcome change for fashion's elite including Anna Wintour who, recalling Ford's appearance on the fashion scene, wrote in 2004, "When I think back to the early 90s, when he first arrived on my radar screen, fashion was buried deep in the shapeless layers of the horrible grunge look … Along came Tom with his low-cut hipsters and his slinky jersey dresses, and grunge was sent scurrying off back to Seattle."

Moving away from the previous year's collection and its celebration of disco colour, 1996 saw suits and jackets in monochromatic colours: sleek black leather and city pinstripe, or all white with neutral accents. The only exceptions were Ford's iconic velvet tuxedos, in red and deep blue. Coats were long and tailored, or otherwise oversized, and made from luxurious fur, and blouses were again slashed to the waist – a Tom Ford trademark – and tucked into hipster trousers, this time accessorized with would what become an iconic Gucci accessory, the skinny belt. Gold hardware was everywhere and became a feature that would be long associated with the brand. The evening wear section of Ford's show saw model upon model in slinky white jersey dresses with sexy cutout features, accessorized with gold belt buckles or with gold fastenings on the peepholes.

Despite the overt sexiness of Ford's designs there was still an androgynous element to his clothes, with similar tailored suits and velvet tuxedos created for both men and women, and all models wore the bottom-skimming hipster trousers. This early blurring of gender-specific dressing set a precedent for how the Gucci brand would evolve even after his departure, with his successors Frida Giannini and, in particular, Alessandro

OPPOSITE The interlocking-G motif was essential to the Gucci brand and all the label's head designers reworked it in their own style. This tailored coat, worn by model Stella Tennant for Spring/ Summer 1997 over a fitted black dress accessorized with razor-sharp heels, is a perfect example of Ford's take on the logo.

Michele pushing the boundaries of androgyny and non-gender specific dressing much further.

As well as the clothes themselves, Ford's shows had a sense of theatre about them that enhanced the feeling that one was watching a louche nightclub scene. He used spotlights to pick out the models as they paraded down the catwalk, explaining that, "I decided to kill the backlighting and put the clothes under a spotlight because I wanted to control the room." Accompanied by a sensual soundtrack, the overall effect shouted "sex". During the following seasons Ford's designs became even more risqué, with models appearing almost naked in barely-there clothes, and in 1997 he famously debuted the Gucci G-string. Worn on the catwalk by almost-naked male and female models alike, the skimpy string underwear, held together by a metallic interlocking-G Gucci logo, was in fact a bikini bottom, but inspired a line of designer lingerie that is still popular today. (In 2018, Kim Kardashian posted an Instagram shot of herself in an original 1997 G-string, which gained her well over two million likes.)

Ford's collections, until he left the brand in 2004, built on his landmark 1996 offering, with 1997 and 1998 continuing to feature plenty of bare skin under navel-skimming satin shirts and cut-away sparkly tops, along with evening wear made from transparent fabrics topped by oversized glam-rock-colourful furs and sexy animal prints. By the end of the 90s, Ford was gradually starting to add more colour and flounces, harking back to the famous floral prints of Gucci's earlier heyday. But even in what might be called classic outfits, the skirts, tops and dresses were figure-hugging, slashed to the waist or semi-transparent, with logo G-strings peeking cheekily out from low-cut hip-huggers. In all of Ford's collections, the 1970s nostalgia was never far beneath the surface, and in his 2002 collection, models in oversized sunglasses and Halston-era gowns continued to channel the Studio 54 vibe.

OPPOSITE Jodie Kidd and Georgina Grenville model in the Gucci Autumn/ Winter 1997 ready-to-wear show. Both looks feature Ford's signature skinny belt.

RIGHT By the end of the 1990s Ford was playing with a looser style of clothes but the sensuality always remained. These purple harem trousers, heavily embroidered with Swarovski crystals and worn sexily low on the hips, were such a statement that Madonna wore them to the 1999 Grammy Awards.

OPPOSITE Ford upped the aspirational glamour of the Gucci brand by using the hottest supermodels for his catwalk shows. Here Gisele Bündchen models a luxe fur coat for Autumn/ Winter 1999.

Ford's position as Creative Director of the whole of Gucci gave the brand a cohesive look that proved very successful. A large part of this came from the label's advertising campaigns, which Ford directed from 1995 onward in collaboration with photographer Mario Testino and stylist Carine Roitfeld. Roitfeld's particular brand of sexy European chic – which later saw her become the hugely successful editor of French *Vogue* – inspired Ford, who saw her as both a consultant but also a muse.

The advertising imagery that the team created began reasonably tamely with a campaign featuring model Amber Valletta, hip thrust out in a half-unbuttoned electric blue satin shirt and velvet

LEFT As a young man, newly arrived in New York in 1979, Ford became a regular at the famous Studio 54 nightclub, and 70s disco glamour was something that would continually influence his designs. Bianca Jagger, who epitomized the style of the club, became a longtime friend of Ford, seen here with the designer attending the CFDA Fashion Awards in 1997.

RIGHT Sex and
glamour will always
define Ford's
creations such as this
python-print cutaway
swimsuit worn by
model Aurelie Claudel
in the Spring/Summer
2000 show.

LEFT Model Jacquetta Wheeler wears a shimmering lilac asymmetric dress complemented with bright pink tights and strappy block-heeled sandals in Ford's Spring/Summer 2000 show in Milan. The collection marked a return to the designer's beloved 1970s disco glamour.

OPPOSITE Ford was never afraid to push boundaries, often with sexual connotations. This sportswear look, worn by model Jacquetta Wheeler for Spring/Summer 2000, pairs a bondage-style bikini top with side-slit silky running shorts and strappy high-heeled gold sandals.

LEFT Accessories have always been essential to the Gucci story and by Spring/Summer 2004, Ford's penultimate collection for the label, the designer upped the decadence quotient, presenting luxury bags such as this fringed metallic evening bag with an emerald green serpent clasp.

OPPOSITE Expanding the sales of accessories was crucial to the success of Gucci, and Ford oversaw striking advertising campaigns all with a subtle edge that infused the brand with sensuality. This sunglasses ad is simple yet effective with the model's parted lips and the Gucci gold emblem becoming the focal points of the image.

GUCCI

LEFT This deeply cutaway, bronze metallic chainmail swimsuit worn by model Julia Stegner for Spring/Summer 2004 is the kind of barely-there outfit that epitomizes Ford's love of slightly trashy glamour.

hipster trousers – the same outfit Madonna wore to the MTV awards that year. Backed by male models, the feel is sultry but nothing compared to the aggressively sexual, sometimes shocking campaigns that would follow.

For Gucci's fashion campaigns, big-name models including Georgina Grenville and Kate Moss appeared in various sexual poses, being groped by or posing entangled with male models. Nudity was commonplace, both for men and women; shirtless male models posed unbuckling their Gucci belts or, in lingerie ads, appeared lying face-down on the beach wearing nothing but the iconic Gucci G-string. And in 2003 Carmen Kass appeared pulling down her Gucci underwear in front of a male model to reveal pubic hair shaved into the Gucci G.

It is of course important to remember that in the late 1990s and early part of the 2000s there was no live-streaming of fashion shows, and the first glimpses of a designer's new collection would come from the advertisements in the fashion magazines' influential March and September issues. Ford pushed his team to the limits to create brand-defining images that reached new heights of creative accomplishment. In an interview with the *Independent* newspaper in 2008, Mario Testino recalled this era, explaining how "advertising campaigns became more exciting than editorial. When I started doing Gucci with Tom Ford, he pushed me to new heights."

Ford generated much debate with his use of controversial advertising for Gucci and also for Yves Saint Laurent, which was by then owned by the Gucci group and with Ford also designer-in-chief. Some ads were so controversial that they were banned by the UK's Advertising Standards Authority – most famously the 2000 Yves Saint Laurent Opium fragrance advertisement featuring a nude Sophie Dahl reclining provocatively, eyes closed and wearing nothing but gold stilettos and jewellery, again styled by Carine

RIGHT This elegant black satin frame bag designed by Ford encompasses many of Gucci's heritage motifs including the bamboo handle and floral pattern.

RIGHT Ford played with the traditional Gucci stripe, experimenting with different colourways including this striking purple and yellow alligator version with enamel dragon closure and bamboo strap.

RIGHT These patent black leather spike heel shoes with studs, designed by Ford in 2003, hint at the powerful dominatrix that so often lurks beneath the outfits in the designer's collections.

Roitfeld. The tactic might have aroused much criticism but, as they say, there is no such thing as bad publicity, and there is no denying that it worked. This was an era when achieving bodily perfection became as much a status symbol as wearing the latest designer label, and Ford managed to fuse the two ideals to make Gucci irresistible to a new generation of shoppers.

When asked in an interview to sum up his legacy for Gucci, Ford replied, "I think I brought back hedonism, a certain kind of ostentatious fashion … a certain sexual glamour." This raw sexuality dramatically increased the appeal of the Gucci brand, coveted not just for its iconic accessories but for its clothes too. And the strong celebrity associations with the brand, thanks to Ford's magnetic personality and social cachet, helped. In an interview with fashion critic Bridget Foley, Ford explained, "Madonna went out in our hip-huggers and our loafer sales went up. Now, here were pinstriped suits that started to sell, that everyone from 30 to 70 could wear. I am a commercial designer and I am proud of that; I have never wanted to be anything else. This gave other people an inkling of what I always knew – that we could really sell clothes."

In 2004, having resurrected the Gucci brand and built an empire that now included Yves Saint Laurent, Balenciaga and Bottega Veneta – plus recent acquisitions of young and exciting designers Stella McCartney and Alexander McQueen – Domenico De Sole left the brand, intending to retire. Ford was earmarked as his successor as CEO, but in a surprise move the designer announced he was also leaving. Rumours surfaced of a rift between Ford and luxury goods conglomerate PPR, which had a controlling stake in the Gucci Group, with PPR claiming Ford wanted too much money. But the designer denied the charge, instead telling *Women's Wear Daily* that "money had absolutely nothing to do with it at all. It really was a question of control." Regardless of why he left, the split was acrimonious to the extent that when the Gucci Museum opened in Florence in 2011, Ford's legacy was strangely diminished, with some exhibits not featuring his work at all. It was only in 2016 after Alessandro Michele, a huge admirer of Ford, took charge of the brand that Ford's massive contribution to the story of Gucci was included.

After leaving Gucci, Ford started his own eponymous label, luring his long-time business partner De Sole from retirement to become chairman of Tom Ford International. The dream team was back in action and Ford's new venture proved as successful as his tenure at Gucci. Meanwhile the role of head of creative design at Gucci was taken over by Frida Giannini, who had worked for alongside Ford at Gucci for two years and who – along with her husband Patrizio Di Marco, who first headed up Bottega Veneta before becoming CEO of the Gucci Group in 2009 – took the label forward.

OPPOSITE Over the last few decades Gucci has actively supported a number of charitable causes through fashion shows and one-off garments. Ford has always been an ardent campaigner for AIDS charities and in 1997 posed for a series of portraits in support of the annual Los Angeles AIDS Project gala.

LEFT In February 2004 Ford takes the applause at his emotional last show for Gucci. His departure marked the end of a defining era for the house.

Frida Giannini

A STREAMLINED GLOBAL BRAND

Frida Giannini is in many ways the quintessential modern Gucci woman. Impeccably groomed, slim, with long, honey-blonde hair, sharply parted at the centre, Giannini is sexy but understated, with a sophisticated style that favours fitted black dresses, elegant trousers and silk tops, paired with Gucci's strappy sandals.

B orn in Rome in 1972, her father was an architect, her mother a professor of art history and, as a middle-class Italian girl growing up in the 1980s, she was part of a pivotal generation. When asked about her influences as a young woman, she cites a wide variety including the sexy romance of Fellini's *La Dolce Vita*, the glamour and gender fluidity of David Bowie, and the nostalgia of *Breakfast at Tiffany's,* all of which were reflected in different ways during her decade-long tenure as head of Gucci. As part of the pre-internet generation, she understood analogue, yet was nevertheless primed to embrace a new world of digital fashion and social media while always acknowledging the importance of a brand's heritage.

OPPOSITE In many ways Giannini embodies the Gucci ideal, always perfectly groomed and elegantly dressed. Here she walks the runway after her Spring/Summer 2007 show wearing one of the Flora printed dresses from the collection.

After studying at the Academy of Costume and Fashion in Rome, Giannini joined the Italian fashion house Fendi in 1997, where she worked on ready-to-wear for three seasons before being promoted to the design of leather goods. Her time at Fendi coincided with the launch of the wildly successful Baguette handbag, one of the first it-bags and one of the products that made Fendi so attractive to the luxury giant LVMH, which subsequently bought the family-run firm. In 2002 Tom Ford hand-picked Giannini and brought her, aged just 24, to Gucci, where she worked as head of design for handbags and accessories until 2004. Ford's abrupt departure saw Giannini promoted to head of accessories, alongside Alessandra Facchinetti who oversaw womenswear, and John Ray who took control of menswear. Just two years later, after an unremarkable couple of collections by Facchinetti, who left in 2005, Giannini took over both womenswear and menswear, as well as store design and all advertising and communication, giving her almost total creative control of the Gucci brand.

After the massive commercial and creative success Ford had achieved during his years at the helm of Gucci – along with the fact he was a fashion celebrity compared to the barely known Giannini – the pressure was on, and it took several years for the young designer to make her mark. For her 2006 Autumn/Winter collection, Giannini seemed to be mimicking Ford with a glam-rock collection full of the 1970s inspired shapes and throwback 90s metallic accessories – including platform shoes with the identical "car paint" high-shine finish that Ford had used in his first collection. Looking more closely, however, Giannini's own influences, notably that of David Bowie and his boundary-pushing sense of style, were beginning to surface. "I was thinking of David Bowie and the way people played with their image to be something different every time they went out in the 70s," she said.

RIGHT & ABOVE One of Giannini's biggest successes was the relaunch of the Jackie bag labelled the New Jackie, shown here in both classic tan leather and Giannini's relaunched Flora print in purple leather and canvas.

LEFT Simple elegance is one of the defining characteristics of Giannini's design, exemplified here in this outfit from Pre-Fall 2010 comprising a brown silk top and tailored wide trousers with tan coat and matching accessories.

OPPOSITE For Gucci's 70s-inspired Autumn/Winter 2011 collection Giannini cited Anjelica Huston as an influence, taking the brand straight back to the Studio 54 days of Ford's collections. Here Joan Smalls wears a flowing turquoise chiffon gown with textured floral stole.

The show was in marked contrast to the many other designers showing in Milan that season, where a new restrained and sombre mood prevailed. But the party was still going strong at Gucci, with plenty of glitzy gold and purple, oversized fur, and sequin-covered fabrics. Reviews, however, were mixed, with fashion commentators unsure whether they liked the label's new creative head.

But by the following year Giannini was beginning to move away from Ford's super sexed-up 70s disco-fever designs, and was instead beginning to look back to Gucci's heritage for womenswear as well as accessories, something that would become a trademark of her leadership of the brand. For the label's 85th anniversary, the designer explained, "I've been thinking about the early 60s, and a few things from the archive." Although *Vogue's* Sarah Mower opined that the collections was less about honouring Gucci's heritage and more about trying to increase the brand's appeal to a younger audience, especially with a random scattering of folksy, girly dresses. Mower further criticized the lack of cohesion in the show as a whole, complaining that "Giannini needs to learn what's for retail racks, and what makes a concise statement in a show".

As the last few years of the decade progressed, Giannini began to noticeably pare down the flounces and ethnic, bohemian accents that had permeated her 2007 and 2008 shows. She presented a carefully curated set of outfits from which *Vogue* deduced that "Frida Giannini is from a different generation than Milan's other female designers, and she sees fashion from a more pragmatic standpoint. Gucci now is a clearly segmented, businesslike collection with no pretence of being anything other than hip, immediately understandable clothes for a young global audience."

RIGHT Though often criticized for changing direction too suddenly, Giannini ignored critics and stuck to her guns. Here model Joan Smalls wears an outfit from her Spring/Summer 2011 collection full of colour blocking in bold, fresh colours.

LEFT Menswear is just as important to Gucci as womenswear, and Giannini always offered subtly fashionable, expensive-looking classic Italian designs such as this double-breasted white suit accessorized by loafers and sunglasses.

RIGHT The Gucci Guccissima embossed leather pattern, shown here on a laptop bag, was designed by Giannini in 2006 and has become a modern classic.

Giannini's strength has always been knowing Gucci's clientele, and in this 2009 collection she exhibited how her priority was to cover all her customer bases. Streetwear was offset by delicate party dresses, and tropical-print shirts sat beneath sharply tailored, boyish suits. This narrow silhouette was named the "Frida" and the slim-cut trousers have become another Gucci signature. The new, focused collection coincided with Giannini moving Gucci's design studio from Florence to Italy's livelier capital, Rome, her home city and one she felt better represented Gucci's new ethos. "Florence is such a small city. The guys in my team, they are young, they need to go out, meet people. Rome has beautiful light, friendly people, a wonderful lifestyle."

Similarly, the Gucci boutiques, also under Giannini's remit, were redesigned as wide, open spaces, filled with natural light, warm wood, and amber glass fixtures and fittings. The stores, like the brand, blended modernity with heritage, projecting status and luxury but also a cool, hip youthfulness.

As the decade turned, Giannini grew in confidence. While retaining the sensuality of Ford's era, so essential in redefining the Gucci brand, Giannini gradually abandoned the overt sexuality and louche hedonism that so defined Ford's collections. Her Spring/Summer 2010 collection went in a new modernist direction with an almost sci-fi edge. White multi-strap and cutaway dresses and mesh tops had a bondage vibe that Ford would have been proud of, but the overall effect was cleaner and bolder, with a feminist assertiveness. As always, heritage accents abounded, with large belts fastened by a variant on the Horsebit and, most importantly, the handbag of the season, a reworking of the old hobo bag named for Jackie Kennedy, now labelled the "New Jackie".

Originally an accessories designer, Giannini has contributed hugely to the evolution of the Gucci it-bag by reworking classics from the label's archives into new, fresh designs. One of her earliest successes was with Gucci's iconic Flora print, first commissioned by Rodolfo Gucci for Grace Kelly in 1966. Giannini resurrected it in 2004, producing a range of vibrantly colourful yet nostalgic canvas bags, which hit the stores as part of the 2005 Cruise collection. The Flora had been somewhat forgotten alongside the other heritage motifs so prevalent on Gucci accessories: the double-G fastening, the Horsebit embellishment and the green–red–green woven stripe. Although Ford had used elements of floral design in some of his later collections, it was Giannini who revived the actual Flora pattern, cementing its importance. Since then Giannini has constantly revisited the print, on handbags, scarves and clothing, naming a fragrance after it in 2009, and even using it for menswear in her Spring 2013 Resort collection.

In 2006 Giannini designed another instant classic in the form of the Gucci Guccissima. Literally translating from Italian

OPPOSITE The throwback to the seventies for Autumn/ Winter 2011 led to some of Giannini's most memorable designs, including this striking belted fur-trimmed suede coat.

94 FRIDA GIANNINI

as "most Gucci", this version of the original double-G print was embossed onto butter-soft leather and became one of the designer-label-obsessed 2000s' most popular logo bags, rivalled only by the updated "New Jackie" bag in 2009 with its instantly recognizable slouchy style. Similarly, Giannini's final collection for the fashion house, Spring/Summer 2015, saw the Bamboo handbag and the Gucci stripe all given the Frida makeover, with yet another modern twist on the psychedelic 1970s.

It was this skill, raking the archives for Gucci classics and updating them for a new audience, that so defined Giannini's time as designer-in-chief. And for the most part it worked, even if she will not be remembered as a designer as exciting as either Ford before her, or her successor Alessandro Michele. In an interview with *Dazed* magazine in 2012, Giannini was asked what she felt defined contemporary Italian fashion and her answer succinctly sums up her approach to design at Gucci: "Duality: the ability to look ahead without losing sight of the past."

The 2011 show, marking Gucci's 90th anniversary, saw a massive injection of the label's old glamour. Citing Studio 54's finest, Anjelica Huston, as one influence, Giannini also named Florence Welch of Florence and the Machine as her muse. (Gucci designed many of the outfits Welch wore on tour and the singer subsequently became an ambassador for the brand under Michele.) The collection, firmly back in the 1970s, was a riot of unexpected colour and texture: aquamarine, scarlet, citrine, burgundy and violet joined velvet blazers, fur-collared coats and feather-trimmed fedoras, with just a little bit of traditional Gucci sex appeal in the shape of a slim, black pencil skirt. Evening wear was made up of long, draped chiffon gowns, the inspiration for which the designer

OPPOSITE Music has always been a huge inspiration to Giannini, who has a personal collection of over 8,000 vinyl records. Here she is pictured with musician Nick Rhodes at a private dinner in New York in 2007 where Mariah Carey and Jon Bon Jovi were also present. The designer was so thrilled to meet the Duran Duran singer that she even serenaded him with one of the band's hits.

attributed to Florence Welch, although, as *Vogue* pointed out "they wouldn't have looked out of place on Angelica circa 1970-something, either".

Of course, music has always been important to the Gucci brand, both as part of the staging of shows and through associations with pop stars such as Madonna, but for Giannini, who admits to a personal collection of over 8,000 vinyl records, it is an inspiration, "Music, much like film, is such a vibrant part of today's culture: It frequently provides inspiration for my work."

RIGHT China is fast becoming another lucrative new market for Gucci and other aspirational brands, and in April 2012 Giannini staged her first show in Shanghai.

OPPOSITE Giannini is credited with resurrecting the 1960s Flora print and bringing it to a modern audience. This large canvas tote bag is a beautiful example.

98 FRIDA GIANNINI

LEFT Giannini's
Spring/Summer
2012 show, full of
beautiful architectural
shapes inspired
by the Chrysler
building of the 1920s,
coincided with the
90th anniversary of
Gucci. However, the
designer insisted that
her art deco-inspired
collection had nothing
to do with the 1921
founding of the brand.

LEFT For her Autumn/ Winter 2013 show Giannini sent models down the catwalk in gloriously embellished evening gowns full of sequins and feathers in wing motifs on top of black mesh. The sensual glamour harked back to the days of Ford.

OPPOSITE Giannini's strong relationship with UNICEF included appointing the singer Rihanna to star in an advertising campaign to benefit the charity. Here the designer is shown with Madonna and Rihanna attending the launch of the Tattoo Heart Collection by Gucci in New York in 2008. Twenty-five per cent of the proceeds from the collection went to the charity.

LEFT The retro feel in Autumn/Winter 2013 was heightened with clothes as skin-tight as Ford would have designed them, including this houndstooth waistcoat and trousers in black and powder blue, with oversized jacket with sunglasses completing the power-woman look.

OPPOSITE Giannini's focus on keeping every bit of Gucci's customer base happy led to some reviewers saying that her shows lacked cohesion. In Spring/Summer 2013, however, she expertly managed the balance, offsetting colourful daywear with monochrome evening wear such as this striking dress.

LEFT A big fan of floral prints in general, Giannini frequently used the motif in her designs as shown here in this black suit patterned with oversized pink and purple leaves.

From David Bowie's Ziggy Stardust to Eugene Hütz, the frontman for gypsy punk band Gogol Bordello, whose Cossack style permeated Giannini's 2008 and 2009 menswear shows, musicians both inspired and collaborated with the designer. In 2008 singer Rihanna performed at a New York Fashion Week Gucci–UNICEF fundraiser. Shortly afterward, Giannini announced that the global superstar would be appearing in an advertising campaign to benefit the charity, wearing limited edition Gucci designs that would be sold, with 25 per cent of sales going to UNICEF. This connection to the world of music and its stars would continue during the next decade as Giannini handed over the reins of Gucci to Alessandro Michele.

Giannini's final few years at Gucci included overseeing the opening of the Gucci Museum at the end of 2011, showcasing not only iconic pieces from the House of Gucci's archives but also work by contemporary artists, as well as a series of breakaway collections including her 2012 Spring/Summer show with its art deco theme and strong, architectural shapes. Colours were monochromatic black and white, or sharply-drawn blocks of green, mustard and white. It was a departure for the designer, but, as always, the collection was eminently wearable off the catwalk, too.

Giannini has always blended the old and the new at Gucci – her final few collections included revisiting the 60s and 70s as well as offering for Autumn/Winter 2014 a pared-down and less overtly glamorous collection. The press were mixed in their opinions, but Giannini was philosophical when she reflected on her critics, in a *Guardian* interview in 2011: "For winter I did 70s and it's 'too much from the archives', and then for summer I did 20s and people say 'she's forgotten about the archives'. Believe me, it can be frustrating … But you can't listen too much. I have a strong point of view, and it's important that I fight for my ideas."

It is this strength of character, and determination to push through regardless, that marked Giannini's leadership of Gucci alongside CEO Patrizio di Marco, with whom she started a romantic relationship when he joined Gucci in 2008. Creatively, both in her collections and for Gucci's advertising campaigns, she has been accused of playing it safe, taming the in-your-face sexuality of Ford and preferring to rework the past. "The Gucci of di Marco and Giannini is more intent on rediscovering its traditions than creating scandal," wrote Italian journalist Daniela Monti.

The relationship of Gucci's designer-in-chief and CEO has partly been blamed for the brand's declining sales which eventually led to both di Marco and Giannini leaving the fashion house. Rumours that other members of the design and business team felt sidelined and kept in the dark when key decisions were being made, culminated at the end of 2014 when di Marco left involuntarily. A leaked staff memo obtained by the *New York Times* made it clear that the businessman did not want to go and blamed enemies within the company for forcing him and Giannini out: "Against my will, I leave my cathedral uncompleted. It's a pity I won't be able to see how this beautiful story would have continued." (The power couple had a daughter in 2010 and finally married just a few months after being ousted from Gucci, Giannini seeming to deliberately snub her former employer by choosing a Valentino dress.)

Although Giannini was given the chance to stay and see her final collection onto the catwalk in February 2015, she departed in January, leaving head of accessories Alessandro Michele just a week to pull together the menswear collection.

RIGHT Giannini has rightly been called a very Italian designer, exemplified in her Spring/Summer 2013 show where Riviera colours mixed with 60s prints, all perfectly coordinated with matching accessories and oversized sunglasses, could have come straight off the backs of Europe's original jet set.

LEFT Global expansion into Asian markets has seen Gucci grow to be one of the world's leading luxury brands. This film noir outfit accessorized by glamorous fur stole and fedora-style hat was part of a collection showcased in Seoul in 2011.

OPPOSITE For the Spring/Summer 2013 menswear collection Giannini offered a similar 60s Italian Riviera lifestyle look complete with patterned jacket, white chinos and Gucci Horsebit loafers, worn barefoot of course.

Again, surprising the fashion world, the relatively unknown Michele was announced as Giannini's successor, with Anna Wintour commenting shortly after meeting him, "He was eccentric, a little bit eccentric, but charming." Her words could not have been truer, and over the coming years, Gucci would be transformed once again under the patronage of Michele's wild and flamboyant genius.

Alessandro
Michele

A
FASHION
VISIONARY

"Those who are truly contemporary are those who neither perfectly coincide with their time nor adapt to its demands ... Contemporariness, then, is that relationship with time that adheres to it through a disconnection."

– Italian philosopher Giorgio Agamben,
quoted in notes left on the seats at
Alessandro Michele's debut show

At the beginning of 2015, after the ousting of designer-in-chief Frida Giannini and her partner, CEO Patrizio di Marco, Gucci was struggling. Sales had slumped, and Giannini's tactic of producing clothes and accessories to please every possible Gucci customer had seemed to backfire, creating the general consensus that the brand had lost direction. Added to this was the overall zeitgeist, which by 2015 was less about conspicuous consumption and status symbols and more about a subtle anti-consumerism. Luxury brands could no longer count

OPPOSITE A look from Alessandro Michele's Resort 2019 collection, shown in the Alyscamp burial ground in Arles, France. Show notes described the models as "widows attending grave sites, kids playing rock 'n' roll stars, and ladies who aren't ladies."

on an ostentatious logo being enough to sell their products, and Gucci's competitors were already relying more on their creativity and craftsmanship than just their names.

As was the case in the 1980s, before Tom Ford arrived at Gucci, the brand was in dire need of a change of direction and a fresh eye. Various contenders were mentioned in the fashion press, including Riccardo Tisci and Peter Dundas from rival luxury goods conglomerate LVMH, and British stylist Katie Grand, who had been brought in by Giannini to stage the Spring/Summer 2015 collection in a last-ditch attempt to up the hip quotient. Even Ford was in the mix, although his return to the fashion house was always unlikely. But to everyone's surprise the job was given to Alessandro Michele, a man little known outside the company, who was currently working as Giannini's associate designer.

The appointment was made by new CEO Marco Bizzarri, rumoured to be the one to have fired Giannini, who he found it hard to get along with. Bizzarri, who had previously worked as CEO at Stella McCartney and Bottega Veneta, definitively rejected Giannini's overemphasis on the past, saying in a 2018 interview for *Fast Company* magazine, "The company was really losing speed and was a little bit dusty. There was too much emphasis on heritage. I wanted to move the company to be more inclusive, more joyful, full of more energy."

Bizzarri could not have chosen better – there are few individuals who epitomize joy and energy more than Michele – and although acknowledging that heritage was still important, it needed to be instinctive rather than through the meticulous scouring of the label's archives. Gucci needed a designer who could become the physical embodiment of the brand and Michele fit the bill. As Bizzarri explained, "Why should I look for someone else when he can translate the heritage – and when the values of Gucci are in his veins?"

OPPOSITE Michele's debut collection for Gucci was menswear Autumn/Winter 2015, which he completely redesigned in just five days after Giannini's sudden departure. From the very beginning the designer blurred gender boundaries, opening the show with long-haired model Hugo Goldhoorn wearing a red silk pussy-bow blouse.

Michele is a striking-looking man, with Messiah-like, long, flowing black hair and matching beard, and his love of heels and eccentric dress sense give him an impressive presence. His flair for theatrical design and the cinematic quality of his catwalk shows come as no surprise when you learn that the designer, who was born in Rome in 1972, studied costume design at Rome's Academy of Costume and Fashion. He also credits his mother, who worked as an assistant to a Rome film executive and "was really obsessed with American movies and cinema. For her it was like a religion." His hippy, nature-loving father, on the other hand, was "a bit of a shaman, with long hair and a beard". Many of the totemic motifs that have come to adorn Michele's designs can be attributed to his father's influence.

Despite his talent for theatre and costume design, Michele decided that fashion would be a more appealing career choice, and he worked first for Fendi (as did Giannini). There he was taken under the wing of Karl Lagerfeld, until Michele joined Gucci's design studio in London in 2002 at the invitation of Ford. He went on to work in a number of design roles at Gucci, rising through the ranks to head up accessories and become one of Giannini's closest design assistants.

OPPOSITE While some of Michele's eclectic creations might be seen as brilliant but hard to wear off the catwalk, others are simply elegant and beautifully designed such as this long dress with its colourful starburst and floral-patterned coat with kimono sleeves.

Michele had already given the fashion world a taste of what he was capable of when he stepped in to salvage the Autumn/Winter 2015 menswear show in just five days, following the abrupt departure of Giannini. Just days later his appointment as designer-in-chief was announced. A month after that he presented his debut womenswear show, which was an immediate hit. As American *Vogue*'s Hamish Bowles put it, "In that single collection he reset the dial at the house, introducing a quirky runway cast wearing gender-neutral clothes that drew on his passion for eclectic vintage references and antique accoutrements."

LEFT Model Lea Issarni in a Resort 2018 look as inspired by streetwear as by the Renaissance.

RIGHT Model Unia Pakhomova wears a semi-transparent Grecian-style dress with gold stripes and heavily sequinned silver detail complemented by a headdress modelled on a gold laurel wreath in Michele's historically-inspired 2018 Resort collection shown at Florence's Pitti Palace.

LEFT At the 2016 Met Gala, Gucci dressed Dakota Johnson, Florence Welch and Charlotte Casiraghi. Michele attended in a silver brocade suit.

The show immediately established Michele as a very different designer to either Giannini or Ford. A true modern romantic, his sensuality is infused with emotion rather than the cold, hard sex appeal of Ford's 1990s designs. Likewise, Giannini's poised formality, evoking the image of the haughty lifestyle of the social elite, could not be further from Michele's effusive eccentricity. A self-confessed magpie of all things old and interesting, Michele admitted shortly after his appointment that he is obsessed with antiques and the past. "I'm not interested in the future – it doesn't exist yet – but I'm really interested in the past and the contemporary. My apartment is full of antique pieces, but I put everything together like a modern installation."

Likewise, with his first show, the feel was vintage boho, full of plenty of frills, flounces and florals. Models, both male and female, paraded down the catwalk in pussy-bow blouses, librarian glasses,

OPPOSITE Actor and singer/songwriter Jared Leto, who is often said to look uncannily like the Italian designer, is a good friend and muse to Michele and almost exclusively wears Gucci, often one-off creations made especially for him.

OPPOSITE A dramatic look from the Resort 2019 collection. Constructed from chiffon and marabou feathers, the ethereal gown contrasts with black studded leather accessories.

RIGHT For his 2017 Resort collection, fittingly shown in Westminster Abbey, Michele paid homage to British designers such as Vivienne Westwood with a Union Jack sweater, Queen-like headscarf and handbag and even an appliquéd corgi dog, albeit adorned with a crown of flames.

LEFT Part of Michele's success has been in taking the millennial backlash against ostentatious label flaunting that saw Gucci's profits suffer and giving it an ironic twist. Sweatshirts with "Gucci" emblazoned across the chest are so in-your-face that they are cool again.

OPPOSITE This iconic Gucci black patent Horsebit loafer is given a Michele twist with the addition of a Donald Duck embellishment for Spring/Summer 2017.

floral suits, and sweaters with elaborate bird and flower motifs, and, like the designer himself, they wore numerous vintage rings, but the overall effect is somehow refreshingly contemporary.

Another noticeable departure from his predecessors was the way in which Michele played with proportions: dresses were shapeless and jackets were exaggeratedly oversized, with fur cuffs that ended only just below the elbow. Nothing could be further from the traditional Gucci look, where a body-skimming silhouette was paramount. And while the iconic Gucci elements were still there, it wasn't in quite the sophisticated way that we had come to associate with the brand. For example, a double-G belt sat atop a flared peasant skirt and the sleek Horsebit loafers came backless and lined with kangaroo fur. The overall effect was not as polished as some might have expected from a brand like Gucci, but it expressed a young, playful mood that would come to redefine the house.

Six months later, at the presentation of Michele's Spring/Summer 2016 collection, the fashion world was raving about the newcomer at Gucci. Called on more than one occasion a "fashion Jesus" (appropriately given his long, Messiah-like locks), he really does seem to see visions others don't.

As Sarah Mower put it in British *Vogue*'s critique of his show, "Alessandro Michele is in the spotlight as the Pied Piper of change – a risk-taker and revolutionary who has not so much wiped the slate clean at Gucci as doodled all over it, coloured it in, stuck sequins on it, and tied it up with a grosgrain bow."

His staging, too, had been transformed for his second show. Rather than use the same dark and smoky nightclub setting that so suited Gucci's previous 1970s disco vibe, Michele instead presented models against the backdrop of a disused train depot, the catwalk itself covered in a printed carpet. Models displayed an orgy of colour, print and texture. Fabrics

OPPOSITE Fluidity is key to the Gucci aesthetic under Michele. A model in the Spring/Summer 2017 menswear show wears a floral printed day dress with patent crocodile boxy bag.

OVERLEAF Kaleidoscopic colour and texture in the Spring/Summer 2017 show. Inspired by 1970s nightclubs and Renaissance Venice, the collection was by turns opulent and mournful.

ranged from knitted Missoni-style lurex to floral chiffon and lace, with many wildly varied printed designs. The 1970s references were there, but, speaking backstage, Michele said he had been more influenced by the Renaissance. Most impressive of all was the design team's attention to detail, offering a range of embellishments that left fashion commentators buzzing with excitement. As the designer himself admitted, "It's a big trip!"

Again, not forgetting this was a Gucci show requiring the inclusion of the label's traditional status symbols, Michele showed his knack for the unexpected, including them as a complement to more eclectic garments. For example, a model in a grass-green, semi-transparent, floral lace dress wore a red–green web stripe belt and interlocking-G loafers, and carried a traditional Gucci structured handbag. These bags, in the stiff-framed style favoured by Queen Elizabeth II (or for an apt 1980s reference, Margaret Thatcher), have been one of Michele's great success stories for Gucci. Redesigned in bright colours, embossed with embroidered floral motifs and sequins, or given a street-art touch, he has managed to make them desirable to a whole new generation of Gucci fans.

The year 2015 was a significant one for both Gucci, back on the map thanks to its new designer-in-chief, and for Michele himself, who was named as the recipient of the 2015 International Designer Award, in recognition of his remarkable achievements. Since then the designer has gone from strength to strength, with *Vogue* calling him "the most-copied fashion-diviner on Earth".

In 2016 retro influences abounded, from the sixteenth century right through to the 1980s, with medieval cherubs finding their way onto a striking, printed red silk and Medici-style pearl-trimmed bodices juxtaposed with urban accessories or puffy 1980s sleeves. Always the geek-chic oversized or coloured glasses

OPPOSITE Michele's catwalk creations are incredibly intricate with multiple influences in one. For Spring/Summer 2018 model Nicole Atieno wears an 80s exaggerated-shouldered, bright blue velvet, rose-embossed jacket over a 70s-style blouse with a quilted floral print skirt. Multiple beaded necklaces offset two classic Gucci bags, coloured paste brooch, statement drop earrings and oversized librarian glasses.

were a common accessory, but there was plenty of street style, too, with urban motifs including a Gucci G spray-painted onto biker jackets by New York street artist and musician Trouble Andrew. And in case you were bored, a model then appeared completely colour-blocked in head-to-toe saccharine hues including candy-floss pink, turquoise and canary yellow (actually resembling a giant bird, as the mainstay of the outfit was a feather-like fur coat), but it all worked in the continuity of Michele's strange brilliance.

The Spring/Summer 2017 collection was glitzier, with a more clubby feel, yet continued the 1970s–Renaissance theme and even included a five-inch wedge version of the Venetian "chopine" – a platform shoe worn by fifteenth century ladies, who needed to be elevated well above street level to avoid lakes of sewage and other filth – along with 1970s tweeds and 1980s frothy, ruched cocktail dresses. Michele's attention to detail, and acknowledgment that even his craziest catwalk creations ultimately needed to be wearable, had him include in his platforms a removable flat slipper with a delicate rose-bud printed insole.

Ever evolving, Michele is clearly influenced by many different cultural phenomena: street style, digital media and pop music, to name but a few. His meeting with Elton John, who he now counts as a friend, at the *GQ* Man of the Year Awards, and John's admission that he is a fan of Michele, led to an homage to the legendary musician in the form of a flared, tweed suit accessories with oversized, glittery 1970s glasses. Florence Welch, introduced to Gucci in Giannini's time, was another inspiration, and the singer became an ambassador for the brand in 2016. And, of course, there's Michele's doppelgänger, Jared Leto, who is such a good friend and muse of the designer that he almost exclusively wears Gucci outfits, many of which are one-off creations.

One of the boldest decisions that Michele made, right from

ALESSANDRO MICHELE 133

RIGHT After meeting at the *GQ* Man of the Year Awards in London in 2016, Michele struck up a close friendship with Elton John. He designs exclusive outfits for the singer and finds frequent inspiration for his collections in the star's trademark style, including seventies disco-wear and oversized glitzy glasses.

the beginning of his tenure at Gucci, was to cast both male and female models to appear in all his runway shows and not differentiate between male and female clothes. In fact, his debut show opened with long-haired model Hugo Goldhoorn in a red silk pussy-bow blouse, a brave move from an unknown designer taking over at an historic, global fashion house. And in February 2017 he presented his first combined mens-and-womenswear show to reveal his Autumn/Winter collections.

Of course Gucci is no stranger to androgyny, with Ford embracing slit-to-the-waist satin shirts and the infamous Gucci G-string for both men and women, while Giannini was inspired by the gender-blurring style of Bowie. Michele, however, appropriately in these days of gender fluidity, doesn't see

RIGHT For Gucci's
Autumn/Winter 2018
show Michele pushed
his designs well out
of most people's
comfort zone.
Staged in a series of
operating theatres,
the show featured
several models who
carried versions of
their own heads.

why any clothes should be assigned to one particular gender. For consumers, floral suits might not be such a stretch, but silk babushka scarves and even full-on evening gowns are fair game as men's clothes for the designer. And, as always, Michele has proved prescient, with male celebrities embracing his outfits. Jared Leto memorably turned up to the 2019 Metropolitan Museum of Art's Costume Institute Gala wearing a Renaissance-style red evening gown and carrying a model of his own head as an accessory, an outfit that Michele had designed for him, saying it would make him look like a character from Shakespeare.

But it is not necessary to go to such extremes to recognize how Michele has reshaped men's fashion. Simply allowing men to step away from the safety of traditionally masculine fabrics and colours, instead embracing glamorous textures and vibrant hues including velvets and silks rich with embroidery and embellishment, has redefined what is to be a millennial man. Michele's fans are as widely varied as Roger Federer, Dapper Dan, Sir Elton John and Snoop Dogg. Along with Leto, his most recent fan and muse is British pop star Harry Styles, with whom he has collaborated on designs and in advertising campaigns. As Michele summed it up in an interview with *GQ* magazine, "I think Harry is the perfect expression of masculinity. He is so relaxed in his body, and completely open to listen to himself. He likes to play with dress, with hair … [and] is really in contact with his feminine part. He's sexy and he's handsome."

Even with his clear acceptance of the wide variety of human expression, Michele has not been immune to causing offence. For example, the inclusion of a black balaclava-style jumper in his new collection in 2019 led to accusations of racism. The garment was likened to the once-common practice of blackface

OVERLEAF The full kaleidoscopic brilliance of Michele's design genius can be seen here as the models pose at the end of his Spring/ Summer 2019 show.

OPPOSITE The Autumn/Winter 2018 show also included a model carrying a macabre baby dragon and wearing a long black robe, reminiscent of medieval priests though dotted with crystals.

make-up, which is now rightly seen as racially offensive. The designer immediately issued a heartfelt apology, explaining that the intention was to reference the performance artist and fashion designer Leigh Bowery, who used flamboyant make-up, and that he had not appreciated the racial connotation. The item was removed from sale and subsequently Gucci announced a programme of diversity awareness, with Michele stating, "I hope I can rely on the understanding of those who know me and can acknowledge the constant tension towards the celebration of diversity that has always shaped my work."

Gucci's sales figures confirm that Michele is not just beloved of the fashion crowd, although deservedly he is revered as one of the most creatively remarkable designers for a long time. His ability to poke fun at the grabby status symbol of the 1980s and 1990s has sparked some truly memorable creations, including the ironic "Guccy" logo, printed on sweatshirts atop a sequinned tiger's head and emblazoned on bags, which was an instant hit with the Instagram generation. Michele's collaborations for Gucci, including with the New York Yankees, have helped redefine the brand for a new generation, and Michele's animal motifs – lions, wolves, tigers and serpents – have become as iconic as the red–green–red stripe and double-G logo, both on products and in advertising campaigns. Named brand of the year in 2017 by *The Business of Fashion*, Gucci has outstripped its competitors under a designer-in-chief who doesn't so much push boundaries as refuse to acknowledge they are there. From ignoring gender stereotypes to learning from criticisms on diversity, Michele is more than just a designer, and his fashion is more than just the clothes on the models. As he himself explained, "Sometimes people think that fashion is just a good dress, but it's not. It's a bigger reflection of history and social change and very powerful things."

OPPOSITE Fetish masks with two-inch spikes might seem to be included for shock value only but Michele is fascinated with how we choose clothes to express or disguise parts of ourselves. "A mask is hollow but also full," he said at the press conference after the show for Autumn/Winter 2019.

A Cult Icon

HIGH FASHION
MEETS
STREETWEAR

A huge part of Gucci's success has been the creation
of instantly recognizable iconic items that infuse the
wearer with the brand's identity.

F rom the patenting of the interlocking double-G logo in
the 1930s, through the Horsebit loafers, Jackie O bag and
Flora print of the 1950s and 1960s, to Tom Ford's skinny
double-G belt snaking around hipster trousers, Gucci's products
proudly proclaim who they are. Guccio Gucci's vision for his
brand was of an aspirational luxury goods label that catered to an
elite of aristocrats and film stars, and for the display of a Gucci
status symbol to communicate the wearer's impeccable taste,
style, and above all their wealth. As Frida Giannini found out
to her cost, the smart designer today needs to gear their offering
towards millennials, celebrities and street-style icons in order to
achieve cultural relevance and financial success.

Fortunately for Gucci, with the arrival of designer Alessandro
Michele, the brand's image has morphed once again to become
synonymous with not just wealth but cutting edge cool, too.

OPPOSITE Rapper Gucci Mane took his name from his own love
of the brand and its connotations. He is the face of the Resort
2020 collection.

Michele's design genius, blending his natural leanings towards vintage eclectic with his love of contemporary culture and street style, led immediately to the redesign of signature pieces. For example, his first show revealed a twist on the Horsebit loafer, shorn of its back and lined with kangaroo fur, and his tongue-in-cheek versions of classic bags with liberal sprinklings of sequins and kitsch animal motifs have become instant bestsellers.

Michele had an immediate effect on the desirability of the label, so much so that, as Robin Givhan, fashion critic at the *Washington Post*, explained shortly after the designer's appointment in 2015, old-school Gucci accessories were once again cool. "That's what's been so interesting about what's happening at Gucci," Givhan said. "Alessandro has been able to help revive the whole idea of Gucci, and not just Gucci Spring/Summer '16."

These redesigned accessories have become Gucci's new cult icons and in turn helped boost the company's profits. (With a 2020 revenue target of 10 billion euros within reach, Gucci is close to overtaking Louis Vuitton, currently the world's largest luxury brand.) In particular, Michele has introduced a series of standout bags including the Soho Disco – a relatively minimalist style made from textured leather with an embossed Gucci double-G logo, cross-body strap and oversized tassel detail – and the Dionysus – a larger, structured bag identifiable by its metal clasp featuring two tiger heads. Michele also successfully relaunched the classic Sylvie bag, with its distinctive gold-toned chain and buckle closure, tracing its heritage back to 1969 and the Moon landing. Belts, too, are one of the more coveted of Gucci's accessories, not beyond the dreams of a twenty-something, cost-wise, and in 2019 shopping site Lyst saw 110,000 global online searches a month for the double-G belt in menswear alone.

But it is some of the more outlandish creations of Michele that have really spoken to the young generation, including

RIGHT Gucci has become so popular among the fashion crowd that the logo is often spotted in fashion week street style editorials such as this picture from Milan in 2017.

OPPOSITE The Gucci Soho bag, with its embossed logo on soft leather and trademark tassel, was launched in 2014 and has become one of Gucci's most successful modern icons. It is worn here by actress Emma Roberts.

streetwear emblazoned with cartoons of his pet dogs or with the ironic "Guccy", and bum bags (or fanny packs as they are known in the US) in Gucci's signature print. His eclectic mix of motifs including the double-G turned into a red apple or sequinned flower, embroidered lions and other animals, and lightning bolts, have updated Gucci's traditional accessories into something far more current.

Gucci deserves credit, too, for its social media savvy, including the brand trending on Instagram with a meme created for the launch of a new timepiece campaign and accompanied by the hashtag #TFWGucci (that feel when). Among the humorous images was one of a swimmer wearing a watch, captioned, "When you have Aquagym at 3pm but you need to accessorize your existential angst eternally."

There are other ways, too, in which Gucci maintains its status as the most sought-after luxury brand, in music, for example, especially rap – a 2015 survey for Macy's saw Gucci topping the chart as the most name-dropped brand in hip-hop of the previous 20 years. The brand's name itself has entered the lexicon, becoming a popular slang adjective meaning "cool"

OPPOSITE The limited run of around 600 Gucci Loves New York bags, designed in 2008 as part of a promotion for the opening of the brand's 460,000-square-foot flagship store with all proceeds going to charity, has become a modern cult classic.

RIGHT Shown here in purple quilted velvet the Gucci Marmont Matelasse bag is another modern icon.

LEFT Celebrity fans turn out in their finery on the front row for the Spring/Summer 2020 presentation in Milan. From left: rapper Gucci Mane, actor Keyshia Ka'oir, actor and singer/songwriter Jared Leto, actor Jodie Turner-Smith and iconic tailor Dapper Dan.

or "good", as in "it's all Gucci". And *Urban Dictionary* defines "Guccify" as "to bling out; to add high-end qualities to a product or service (or outfit); to make something overly impressive, expensive, or elaborate."

Michele (who was himself immortalized in rapper Jermaine Dupri's song 'Alessandro Michele') has embraced Gucci's popularity with hip-hop artists and fans, casting Gucci Mane for the 2020 Resort campaign and joining forces in 2017 with Harlem tailor Dapper Dan, who was once sued by Gucci (and other luxury brands) for ripping off their logo in his own unique take on street style, or as he calls it "high-end, ghetto-fabulous clothing". Marco Bizzarri, Gucci's CEO and the man responsible for promoting Michele to designer-in-chief, is determined to maintain the brand's "post-ironic" status and relevance to millennials, something he is already achieving. More than half of Gucci's newly doubled sales in 2018 came from buyers under 35, according to *Business Insider*. And with Michele's never-ending imagination when it comes to innovative, fresh, new fashion, Gucci's ascent seems unstoppable. In an interview with *Fast Company* magazine, Bizzarri again stressed the importance of doing something unique and authentic:

"The point is that if you are able to spontaneously and genuinely talk to millennials in a way that they can see really comes from the heart, you are talking their language … This genuine passion is something that can keep us ahead of the competition. I've read many things about millennials these days saying they are not loyal and switch from one brand to the next. This may be true, but it doesn't apply to us."

OPPOSITE Rapper 2 Chainz wears a Gucci signature Diamante print jacket to the BET Awards in 2018.

INDEX

CREDITS

The publishers would like to thank the following sources for their kind permission to reproduce the pictures in this book.

Alamy: Grzegorz Czapski: 29; /WinkinPink Picture Library 71

Bridgeman Images: 26; /The Advertising Archives 40; /Reporters Associati & Archivi/ Mondadori Portfolio 34t; /Roberto Carnevali/ Reporters Associati & Archivi/Mondadori Portfolio 37

Getty Images: Bettmann 24; /Victor Boyko 152-153; /Vittorio Zunino Celotto 6, 11, 100, 112, 115; /Paolo Cocco/AFP 72; /Erin Combs/Toronto Star 20; /Denver Post 8; / Pietro D'Aprano 118, 119 /Todd Duncan/ Newsday 44; /Estrop/WireImage 126; / Farabola 43; /Terry Fincher 45; /Charley Gallay/Getty Images 146; /Paras Griffin/ WireImage 144; /Horst P. Horst/Conde Nast 36; /Hulton-Deutsch Collection/Corbis 42; / Gerard Julien/AFP 64; /Mansell/The LIFE Picture Collection: 16; /Guy Marineau/Conde Nast 52, 53, 54; /David McGough/The LIFE Picture Collection 33; /Miguel Medina/AFP 131; /Filippo Monteforte/AFP 135, 136; / Antonio de Moraes Barros Filho/WireImage

98-99; /Han Myung-Gu/WireImage 108; / Cornel Cristian Petrus 149; /Jacopo Raule 122; /Bob Thomas/Popperfoto 49; /Venturelli/ WireImage 86, 90, 93, 116, 123, 124, 128-129, 138-139, 141; /Victor Virgile/Gamma-Rapho 104, 106, 109, 125; /Theo Wargo/WireImage 101; /Edward Wong/South China Morning Post 75, 91

Heritage Auctions, HA.com: 9, 19, 27b, 31t, 31b, 74t, 74b, 85t, 85b, 96, 150, 151

Courtesy of Kerry Taylor Auctions: 30, 35

Private Collection: 27t

Shutterstock: 18; /Matt Baron 132; /Michael Buckner/WWD 120; /Domenico Esposito 34b; /Fairchild Archive/Penske Media 59, 66, 77, 82, 86, 89, 94; /Granger 17; /Paul Hurschmann/AP 57; /IPA 46; /Mark Large/ Daily Mail 60, 63; /Cavan Pawson/Evening Standard 67, 68, 78-79; /Reset 70; /Startracks 10, 148, 155; /Ken Towner/Evening Standard 65; /Andrew H Walker/WWD 121; /Wood 69; /Richard Young 134

Topfoto: 14

LITTLE BOOK OF

Dior

First published in 2020 by Welbeck
An Imprint of HEADLINE PUBLISHING GROUP

45

Cataloguing in Publication Data is available from the British Library
ISBN 978-1-78739-377-6
Printed and bound in China

HEADLINE PUBLISHING GROUP
An Hachette UK Company, Carmelite House
50 Victoria Embankment, London EC4Y 0DZ

www.headline.co.uk
www.hachette.co.uk

LITTLE BOOK OF

Dior

KAREN HOMER

WELBECK

Contents

INTRODUCTION

"My dream? To make women happier and more beautiful."
– Christian Dior

In 1947 in Paris – a city still reeling from the Nazi occupation of Europe, where rationing and austerity continued to affect every area of life – an idealistic couturier by the name of Christian Dior had just opened his own fashion house. His first collection was eagerly anticipated, and as models sashayed through the elegant dove-grey rooms of his salon, there was a collective intake of breath. Gone were the square-shouldered, masculine jackets and neat, short skirts of wartime, replaced by perfectly tailored elegant jackets that moulded themselves to the curves of the models; waists were tinier than could be imagined and hips rounded exaggeratedly over skirts that swirled in yards of fabric. It was an audacious debut, immortalized in the words of Carmel Snow, editor-in-chief of *Harper's Bazaar*: "It's quite a revolution, dear Christian! Your dresses have such a new look!" Fashion history was made and the New Look was born.

Despite its creator's untimely death just a decade later, the haute couture house that Christian Dior founded has always stood for glamour, elegance and luxury. The tenets of design that Dior laid down in the beginning – an architectural level of skill in tailoring and craftsmanship, a focus on femininity and making a woman feel more beautiful in his clothes, a clever marriage between the historical influence of fashion

RIGHT Christian Dior sketching in his elegant salon at 30 avenue Montaigne.

and meeting the needs of a modern woman – have endured for more than 70 years. The New Look is still instantly recognizable and is a touchstone for fashion historians and designers alike.

The immensely talented head designers who succeeded Dior, including Yves Saint Laurent, Marc Bohan, Gianfranco Ferré, John Galliano, Raf Simons, and current chief Maria Grazia Chiuri, have respected the designer's intentions while still offering their individuality to the label. Alongside a savvy business team, they have steered the label through the changing world of fashion, from the rise of ready-to-wear and accessories to the brand's global expansion into fragrance and cosmetics. Today, Dior is one of the most successful luxury brands in the world, and its founder is far from forgotten. With the wildly popular retrospective *Christian Dior: Designer of Dreams* shown first in Paris in 2017, and then in London in 2019, the vision of the designer continues to be shared with a new generation.

Early Life

ABOVE Christian Dior's childhood home in Granville, Normandy, as it is today. His beloved flowers inspired a lifelong passion for floral designs and embellishments that endures at Dior to this day.

AN IDYLLIC
CHILDHOOD
HOME

Christian Dior was born on 21 January 1905 in Granville,
a smart seaside town on the coast of Normandy,
and was the second of five children.

His family was wealthy thanks to a fertilizer and chemicals
business founded by his great-great grandfather in 1832.

In his autobiography, *Dior by Dior* (1957), Dior described
their Normandy clifftop home: "like all Anglo-Norman
buildings at the end of the last century … [it was] perfectly
hideous [but] … in a certain sense my whole way of life was
influenced by its architecture and environment". The house
was painted a "very soft pink, mixed with grey gravelling,
and these two shades have remained my favourite colours in
couture". In the linen room, housemaids and seamstresses
worked tirelessly; Dior recalls it was "the place I loved more
than any other … I lingered … absorbed in watching the
women around the oil lamp plying their needles".

As a child, Dior exhibited a passion for flowers and was
happy to spend hours alone among the plants and flowerbeds
or reading *Vilmorin-Andrieux* botanical catalogues. This
interest, inherited from his mother, heavily influenced
his work as a designer: he loved to sketch sitting in his

gardens, and used abundant floral patterns, embroidery and embellishments on his gowns and dresses. His New Look silhouette was designed to represent an inverted flower, and the salons of Maison Dior were always full of grand floral arrangements. The garden and floral theme runs through the company to this day – all the designers to succeed Christian Dior have used floral fabrics and embroidered flowers or petals made from silk, as well as incorporating fresh flowers into catwalk and haute couture shows.

Christian Dior was five years old when his family moved to a grand apartment in Paris. The city was enjoying the final years of the Belle Époque, a golden age before the outbreak of World War I. The young Dior happily absorbed the atmosphere of gaiety and creativity in a period when the arts, theatre and music flourished. Once the war was underway, life was more tense, but Dior wrote of keeping up morale by singing and dancing. He was already showing an interest in fashion when a magazine from Paris arrived,

RIGHT Dior spent hours as a child reading botanical catalogues, sparking a passion for floral print and design.

"announcing that the Parisiennes were wearing short skirts and 'flying boots' … laced up to the knees. Disapproval was unanimous and powerful. All the same, on that very day, each one hastened to order boots and short skirts from Paris by the evening post."

After the end of World War I, a teenage Dior immersed himself in contemporary arts, literature and music, attending private views and patronizing small, exclusive galleries. After finishing school, Dior suggested to his parents that he pursue his interest in architecture and study fine arts. However, they did not feel this would lead to a suitable career and instead enrolled him on a political science course with a view to launching him into a career as diplomat. Nevertheless, Dior pursued his passion for the arts, admiring the new surrealist painters, watching expressionist avant-garde films and spending nights at plays by Anton Chekhov. He was also seduced by the glamour of the Folies Bergère and other lively venues, quickly becoming a fan of performers like the Dolly Sisters and Josephine Baker.

It was soon obvious that a career as a diplomat would not suit the young Dior, so he persuaded his parents to allow him to study musical composition instead. He experimented with expanded tonality and was impressed by composers such as Henri Sauguet, although his parents despaired at the sounds coming out of their drawing room. The cultural life that Dior led during these formative years not only helped develop his personal tastes but also led him to make friends within a wide social circle that would stay with him for life. One of these friends, Jean Ozenne, worked in couture and had an early influence on Dior's future career.

For several years, Dior had managed to postpone his military service because he was still a student, but in 1927 he was finally made to sign up. Declaring himself an anarchist and a pacifist, he refused to join the officers' squad and instead became a second-class sapper in the Fifth Génie de Versailles, a regiment near Paris. Using this time to decide what he was going to do next, Dior proposed that he should

RIGHT Avant garde performers like Josephine Baker were compelling to the young designer and Dior later created outfits for Miss Baker to wear on stage.

open an art gallery, despite his parents' reservations. His father agreed to back Dior on the proviso that his name did not appear on the gallery itself, as to have one's name over a shop door would have been the pinnacle of social shame to his traditional and well-to-do parents. Dior went into partnership with his friend Jacques Bonjean and opened a small gallery that traded in what would become some of the most important painters of the century, including Pablo

Picasso, Henri Matisse, Salvador Dalí and Max Jacob. Dior later commented that if he had kept the stock of paintings, their value would have been incalculable. In 1928, Dior met Pierre Colle, who became a close friend and joined the staff of the gallery.

In 1930, just after the American economic crash sparked the worldwide Great Depression, Dior suffered a series of blows. First, his brother was diagnosed with an incurable nervous disease and his beloved mother, full of grief, faded away and died. Shortly after, at the beginning of 1931, the depression hit France and his father, who had invested heavily in real estate, saw his fortune vanish. With bailiffs arriving at the house to seize any assets they could, Dior moved the family's artworks to the gallery. But Jacques Bonjean's family had suffered a similar fate, and soon the gallery had to close. Dior, determined to keep going, partnered with Pierre Colle to open a new gallery, but artworks had devalued so dramatically that it was impossible to stay afloat, and this too was soon forced to close.

Dior was left virtually destitute. His family had returned to Normandy, unable to afford to live in Paris. Dior himself was forced to share attic rooms with friends. But looking back, he remembered the camaraderie and determination to find small pleasures during these hard times: "For a night, with the help of a few bottles, a piano, and a gramophone we would keep away the mice as we invented fantastic amusements … [including] Charades in fancy dress".

Perhaps inevitably given his peripatetic lifestyle, Dior fell seriously ill and was forced to leave the city for healing mountain air. During the year he spent abroad, Dior began exploring his own creativity. He learned the art of tapestry, worked on his designs and even considering setting up a

workshop. But when he finally returned to Paris, Dior needed a steady job and applied to the fashion house of designer Lucien Lelong. In the interview, he found himself suggesting he would be more useful working on the couture side of the business than in the office. Although Dior wasn't given a job at the time, Lelong would later hire him as a designer.

Fortunately, Dior finally had a stroke of good luck – he was able to sell one of the few paintings he had left, *Plan de Paris* by Raoul Dufy, which he had bought cheaply. This gave him the funds to postpone the need to find a job immediately, as well as to help his family, who were still struggling. At the same time, Jean Ozenne, then a fashion designer before his acting career took off, suggested Dior train as a fashion illustrator. Dior had obvious flair and was soon selling sketches to fashion magazines and dedicating himself to creating dress and accessory designs. Over the next two years, Dior built a reputation for himself as a designer. He found himself a flat and, in 1938, was hired by Robert Piguet as an in-house designer, where Dior was credited with designing the *Café Anglais* dress in houndstooth with a trimming of lace that was much admired that season. It was here that the designer was first introduced to Carmel Snow, the *Harper's Bazaar* editor who would later coin the term "New Look". But before that exciting part of Dior's life could begin, his career was interrupted by the outbreak of World War II, and in 1939, the 34-year-old designer was called up again for military service.

The
War Years

ABOVE Fabric rationing during World War II led to British designer Norman Hartnell releasing patterns for streamlined "utility dresses", which used a bare minimum of cloth. Dior's extravagantly full New Look dresses were a shocking contrast to the austerity of the war years.

FIGHTING
FOR
COUTURE

Christian Dior spent only a year doing military service
and was lucky enough to avoid active combat.

Instead, he was stationed in Mehun-sur-Yèvre in central
France among down-to-earth peasants, wearing wooden
clog-like "sabots" on his feet – far from the rarefied world of
couture. During this time, Dior discovered a love of working
the land and after finishing his military service in 1940, he
rejoined his impoverished family in the South of France.
There, he helped his father and sister Catherine in growing
vegetables, which brought in good money at the market
during a time of food rationing. Dior then received some
incredible news: several pictures that he had sent to America
before the war had been sold. He received a windfall of 1,000
dollars, quite probably some of the last foreign currency to be
allowed into France.

Even outside the cultural centre of Paris, Dior managed
to find himself among an artistic crowd. Despite the
deprivations of war, he socialized with the many Parisians
who had retreated to Cannes, where putting on theatrical
performances was a regular pastime. Dior also continued to
send his fashion sketches to the newspaper *Le Figaro*, where

they were featured in the women's pages. By the end of 1941, the couture houses in Paris had reopened their workshops and Dior decided to return to his design job with Robert Piguet. Unfortunately, Piguet had tired of waiting for Dior to come back and had replaced him. Dior was instead taken on by Lucien Lelong, who ran a larger couture house with an excellent tradition of fine workmanship, which turned out to be a far better training ground.

Dior worked alongside Pierre Balmain at the House of Lelong, one of the few couture houses that remained in France during the German occupation. Other designers, including Mainbocher and Schiaparelli, left for America. Some, like Madeleine Vionnet, closed, never to reopen. Lelong, then the president of the Chambre Syndicale de la Haute Couture, trod a fine line negotiating with the Nazis,

BELOW Christian Dior worked for fashion designer Lucien Lelong 1941–1946, learning a huge amount about haute couture and contributing designs that showed an early version of his New Look.

RIGHT Christian Dior continued to hone his skills as a fashion designer under the tutelage of Lucien Lelong.

who had demanded that the Paris couture houses be moved to Berlin. Germany's plan was to move the couturiers to Hitler's Third Reich, where they would use German dressmakers and essentially become German designers. In 1941, the Chambre Syndicale was inspected and the archives requisitioned. However, the plan to appropriate the tradition of French couture and make the industry German was impractical. As Lelong explained to the Nazis, the fashion houses relied on thousands of artisans skilled in techniques such as embroidery, and it would be impossible to teach a new generation of German workers skills that had been passed down through generations. The Nazis reluctantly acquiesced, allowing the houses to remain open and the couturiers to continue working in Paris, but it was a time fraught with the constant worry that the maisons would be forced to close.

Lelong did manage to remain open during the war, often designing dresses for Nazi officers' wives. After France's liberation, it was suggested that Lelong had been a collaborator. However, at his trial the judge ruled that he had cooperated with the Germans as little as possible – and only in order to save French jobs and the cultural legacy of French couture. In 1945, as Paris fashion was starting to recover, Lelong sent a pared-down collection abroad, including some dresses with nipped-in waists and longer-length skirts. It was a taste of what was to come, and it was almost certainly designed by Christian Dior and Pierre Balmain. Two years later, Lelong was in the audience when Dior showed his legendary New Look collection, which Lelong greatly admired. His protégés had outgrown him, and while Lelong emulated Dior by showing a collection with the New Look silhouette the following year, he closed his couture house in 1948, citing health problems. Dior always spoke fondly of his mentor, acknowledging the skills he had imparted and the freedom he had given Dior to find his way as a designer.

Life in occupied France was a difficult time, and no one fought back harder than Christian Dior's beloved younger sister, Catherine. Despite a 12-year age gap, the siblings were extremely close, and Dior had found his sister a job in Paris, where they lived together before the war. It was there that she fell in love with married shopkeeper Hervé des Charbonneries and, scandalously, started living with him. When he revealed to her that he was a member of the French Resistance, Catherine immediately joined the rebel organization as a spy. But, on 6 July 1944, Catherine was captured and arrested by the Gestapo and detained at Drancy, an internment camp in the suburbs of the city.

Catherine was tortured for information, and when she refused to betray the Resistance, she was shipped by train to Ravensbrück, Germany's largest concentration camp for women. The Dior family never gave up hope that she would return to them, and on 30 April 1945, the Soviet Army liberated the camp at Ravensbrück. Catherine returned emaciated and fragile, part of her irreparably damaged. She received several awards, including the Légion d'Honneur, the highest commendation for military and civil merits. Her strength and patriotism were an inspiration to her brother Christian, and she was his greatest supporter when he launched his New Look.

Despite her role as a muse to her brother – embodying all the strength, humility, and grace he valued so highly in women – Catherine shunned the limelight. She stayed with her lover permanently, helping to raise his children, and spent her life devoted to growing flowers, many of which were used for Dior's fragrances. Appropriately, his first-ever scent, *Miss Dior*, was named for her. After Dior's death in 1957, Catherine got permission for the many flowers sent in tribute from around the world to be laid at the Arc de Triomphe as a mark of respect for his great contribution to French couture. Catherine inherited much of her brother's fabric, furniture and paintings. Upon her death in 2008 at age 91, these belongings were returned to the newly restored Château de La Colle Noire, where Christian Dior once lived.

The
New Look

"IT'S QUITE A REVOLUTION, DEAR CHRISTIAN!"

In 1946, Christian Dior was approached by the extremely wealthy textile magnate Marcel Boussac, who was impressed by Dior's work and wanted a designer to resurrect an old fashion house named Philippe et Gaston.

The offer was tempting. However, Dior refused to work under another's name, insisting that the new house be eponymous. Boussac agreed to back him, and on 16 December 1946, the house of Christian Dior opened its doors at 30 Avenue Montaigne. The designer's eagerly anticipated first collection – the last haute couture show of the Spring/Summer season – was unveiled on 12 February 1947 to a room packed with the upper echelons of Parisian society, alongside the most stylish of the fashion crowd. As the models began to parade the 90 debut looks around the elegant grey-hued salon, the atmosphere was "electric", American *Vogue* editor Bettina Ballard later wrote.

OPPOSITE This iconic image of the New Look has a woman posing elegantly, wearing Dior's peplum "Bar" jacket with its sloped shoulders and tiny waist that flares over the hips to meet a full black skirt – topped with a woven hat.

Journalists around the world were suitably impressed with Dior's debut collection, which quickly graced the cover of American *Vogue*, but it was Carmel Snow, the editor-in-chief of *Harper's Bazaar*, whose words immortalized this daring style: "It's quite a revolution, dear Christian! Your dresses have such a new look!" And so the term "New Look" was coined – and with it, a whole new way of dressing was born.

Dior's tailoring has often been described as having an architectural quality, and his love of beautifully structured garments in the finest cloth is often recognized as his trademark. The expertise of his dressmakers is readily apparent from the meticulous attention paid to the clothes. However, it is important to understand just how revolutionary the New Look was. World War II had ended less than two years previously, and France was still recovering from German occupation. Similarly, in Britain – where Dior was popular, particularly among the upper classes – clothes rationing lasted until 1949. When the New Look first burst onto the scene, it was the exact opposite of the fashion that had come before it, in which shoulders had been squared off, hats had been adorned with flowers and fruit, and shoes had heavy platforms. In contrast, Dior's collection was breathtaking in its pared-back silhouette. The neatly rounded shoulders, curved waist and flared, elegant skirts were fluid yet structured, exquisitely tailored yet flattering and easy to wear. Footwear and millinery were integral to Dior's overall style, and he accessorized his looks with neat heels and sharply drawn hats. The designs that Dior created, although beautiful, were viewed by some as shockingly extravagant. But there were plenty of women for whom the end of wartime austerity could not come soon enough, and buying a New Look suit was one way to signal the start of a new era in fashion.

OPPOSITE Dior's collections, as seen here in 1950, were shown in the elegant, grey-painted salon of his atelier at 30 Avenue Montaigne and always attracted a full house.

LEFT Christian Dior was a talented artist who created beautiful sketches of his revolutionary 1947 New Look dresses.

LEFT A haute couture collection typically showed over 200 designs carefully selected by Dior himself, to be made up by his team of talented atelier artisans.

Christian Dior's first collection presented two distinct silhouettes: the "Corolle", which Dior described in the press notes as "dance-like, very full-skirted, moulded bust and slim waist", and the "En Huit" or "8" line, characterized by the designer as "clean and rounded, the chest is underlined, hollowed-out waist, accented hips". What is obvious in these descriptions is Dior's love of the female form. His clothes were designed to accentuate the curves that were there, and give the illusion of an hourglass figure to those who weren't naturally built that way.

Take, for example, the iconic and monochromatic "Bar" suit that immediately springs to mind when one thinks of the New Look: it has a beautifully tailored ivory silk jacket with a tiny waist flaring over rounded hips and an almost gratuitously full pleated skirt, made from four metres of black wool, that falls to mid-calf. Other suits and dresses from the collection were tailored in the same way. This style, paired with Dior's use of a subdued colour palette, including shades he described as "navy, grey, griege and black", rendered the collection at once modern and nostalgic. The accentuated curves revealed the influence of both Edwardian-era corsetry and the exaggerated, wide skirts of the nineteenth century, yet the look was softened by modern colours and shape – and instantly recognizable as a fashion classic.

Dior's second collection, for Autumn/Winter 1947, was hotly anticipated by the fashion world; would the designer be able to deliver another collection as perfectly curated and innovative as his debut performance? The answer was yes, and the New Look of Autumn/Winter 1947 was pushed to even greater extremes, as American *Vogue* confirmed: "His second collection proves that he is not just occasionally good." The new silhouette continued to exaggerate the

female form, drawing in waists even more tightly, rounding and softening the shoulder to contrast more drastically to the sharp, wide shoulders that had been so popular just a year previously and, if possible, skirts were even fuller. *Vogue* reported "immensely wide, immensely long skirts" and Dior, in his autobiography, recalled using "a fantastic yardage of material [that] … this time went right down to the ankles".

Dior again used a flower analogy as he described how he inserted pleated "petal panels" into long, flared skirts. When an outfit presented a straighter, tubular skirt, the designer paired it with a jacket that had a padded peplum jacket, so the look still gave the illusion of exaggeratedly round hips and focused the eye on the woman's curves. For this cool-weather collection, Dior chose sumptuous, heavy fabrics

OPPOSITE In 1947, many Parisiennes were outraged by the amount of fabric being used in Dior's New Look dresses after wartime fabric rationing, and in protest tried to rip the dresses from the models.

RIGHT This model reclining in Dior's salon – full of elegant furniture and fresh flowers – and wearing a New Look mid-calf dress, offset with a fur-trimmed coat, veiled hat and gloves, epitomizes Dior glamour.

including velvet and brocade, and yet the models moved fluidly in their clothes. Dior spoke of an emotional lightness in this collection too, revelling as it did in liberation from war. He called this era a second "golden age", and believed "when hearts were light, mere fabrics could not weigh the body down."

Always a designer to consider the finished look of his outfit, Dior increasingly placed more importance on accessories. His second New Look collection introduced his signature side-hat, worn jauntily on one side of the head, an elegant twist of hair on the other. Within a few years, it

RIGHT This stunning hussar-style velvet and wool couture suit shows how Dior structured his outfits, juxtaposing a tight waist with full skirt and sleeves. The green accents in the hat, scarf and belt and the textural contrast of black leather gloves and fox-fur muff pull the look together.

RIGHT This silhouette is typical of Dior's New Look, with its nipped-in waist, padded hips and full, flared skirt. The matching hat, gloves and shoes complete the look.

had become essential to the 1950s look. Jewellery, too, was crucial: the designer complemented his evening dresses with brilliantly sparkling statement necklaces.

Over the next few seasons, in the final years of the 1940s, Dior remained true to his groundbreaking silhouette, but there were subtle tweaks that made each new collection as well received as the last. For example, take his 1948 "Zig Zag" and "Envol" lines, the first described by the designer as giving the wearer "the animated look of a drawing"; the second line, translated as "Fly Away", distributed the fullness of the skirt unequally, a difficult design to pull off but one that allowed an increased sense of movement through the exaggerated rise and fall of the skirt.

The focus of Dior's new collections gradually moved from the bosom to the skirt, which became stiffer with the use of backing fabric for an even more structured finish. Even in the daywear outfits, Dior's usual impeccably tailored suits included a "stiffened wing protruding down the back". The "flightiness" that Dior sought with the "Envol" collection was confirmed in his winter "Winged" line, in which movement and volume were achieved with a single, deep inverted pleat in the back and front of dresses and coats. The "wings" were more literal, too, with details including high, pointed collars and exaggerated, pointed cuffs. This was also the season Dior started playing with asymmetric necklines on his evening gowns, to great effect.

RIGHT It is hard to believe now how scandalous Dior's longer-length skirts, with their greater fabric requirements, were in the late 1940s. Skirt lengths remained a defining factor in fashions for decades to come.

ABOUT This black Dior New Look wool melton day dress from 1948 has gently sloped shoulders – in contrast to the square, masculine shoulders of early 1940s fashion – a tiny waist and a full, long skirt. Dior also included details like large pockets, flared cuffs and neck bows.

One of Dior's great skills was to create optical illusions with his masterful cutting, most obvious in the way his outfits give the wearer an exaggerated female form. But he also used other techniques to trick the eye. In 1949, Dior even created a "Trompe L'oeil" line (literally translated as "deceive the eye") that used floating panels, which would swing to give the illusion of fullness, and carefully placed pleats in jackets and dresses. His judicious determinations of where to allow the fabric to fold added fluidity and volume despite the Dior silhouette essentially remaining clean and smooth.

This emphasis on the way Dior's garments were cut and the individual grain of his wide choice of luxurious

LEFT This stylized photograph by Cecil Beaton, of a woman wearing a 1947 New Look black wool dress, sums up the romantic mood of the collection perfectly.

RIGHT This May 1951 shot by Norman Parkinson for American *Vogue* shows just how full and extravagantly pleated Dior's dresses had become by the turn of the decade.

fabrics – including velvet, wool, silk, satin and grosgrain – continued to be of utmost importance to the designer. In his autobiography, he wrote of his final collection of the decade – the "Milieu du Siècle" ("Mid-Century") collection – that "it was founded on a system of cutting based on the internal geometry of the material". By playing with an intersection of straight- and bias-cut panels, which he likened to the crossing of scissors or fanning of windmills, he created a collection that pushed his design skills to dizzying new heights. And so the House of Dior entered the 1950s with a firmly established reputation as one of the most important names in haute couture.

The
House of Dior

EXPANSION INTO AMERICA & GREAT BRITAIN

At the beginning of the 1950s, Christian Dior had been head of his own haute couture house for just three years and had created fashion history with his daring New Look.

His clients included the cream of international society, royalty, and stars of the silver screen – expansion was a natural step for the designer. His first move was to strike licensing deals so that customers could buy the whole Dior "look" and in 1948, he licensed the manufacture of hosiery under his name, soon followed by arrangements for bags, shoes and jewellery. In the same year, he moved into the American market, opening a luxurious ready-to-wear store on New York's Fifth Avenue, as well as selling patterns for Dior garments to big department stores such as Bergdorf Goodman and Marshall Fields in Chicago. Dior would send the pattern, measurements and fabric, and seamstresses

OPPOSITE Christian Dior enjoyed the old-fashioned luxury of the *Queen Mary* ocean liner when he travelled to America after opening a luxurious store on New York's Fifth Avenue in 1948.

ABOVE In 1952, Dior went into business in
Great Britain, producing new designs tailored to
the tastes of English women. Here, he shows a
seamstress how to drape an evening gown.

would copy the dress, which would then be sold, often in an
elegant salon within the store. Though the pieces were not
always as beautifully finished as the haute couture originals,
owning a little bit of Christian Dior at a fraction of the price
of couture was a dream come true for the American middle
classes.

In London, the demand for Christian Dior reached a
fever pitch when journalists covered his debut showing at
the Savoy hotel in 1950, especially when it became known

RIGHT American *Vogue* shows a blue ribbed Dior bathing suit in 1954. Specialized clothing was produced by manufacturers to whom Dior licensed his name and was incredibly popular.

that the glamorous Princess Margaret was a fan. However, other than a few licensed manufacturers who bought the rights to make copies from the toiles produced by the Dior ateliers, very few Dior garments could be bought in Britain. So, in 1952, Dior went into partnership with two clothes manufacturers, Coleman Jeffreys and Marcel Fenez, and Laura Ward, Countess of Dudley, to open C.D. Models (London) Ltd.

RIGHT Dior was a passionate Anglophile who sourced the cloth for his British designs from traditional makers. This model, photographed in the St James's area of London, shows off a tweed sheath coat dress made from heritage fabric.

The Countess of Dudley was a remarkably well-connected woman with an innate elegance and sense of style, which made her the perfect ambassador for Dior's clothes in Britain. As well as being in charge of all press and marketing, she held the important job of selecting which designs would be reproduced at the London ateliers in Maddox Street. This was a responsibility that required a careful balancing of the British woman's sensibilities with Ward's desire to

add a little French *joie de vivre* to her wardrobe. Needless to say, some designs had to be modified in line with what the upper-class Englishwoman found acceptable. By the end of 1954, Dior himself had become more personally involved in Christian Dior London (as it was now known), designing garments specifically for the British market. As an ardent Anglophile, he strongly encouraged the use of British fabrics. Similarly, when entering into licensing agreements for accessories or specialist clothing, Dior almost always chose British companies with a longstanding tradition of fine craftsmanship, like Dents gloves and Lyle & Scott knitwear.

Dior's popularity in Britain continued to grow, through fashion shows and press coverage. The designer, aware of his public persona, was happy to be interviewed about his design process and gave tips on how to dress more elegantly. A wide number of stores now stocked his clothes and accessories with some, like Harrods in London, holding in-store shows that emulated Paris haute couture when a new collection was released; Harrods even had its own "Dior Room" where customers could view all the latest designs and accessories. The love affair with Dior and his elegant clothes, so suited to the aristocratic classes, continued, and news of his sudden death in 1957 was received with great sadness.

Nevertheless, in November 1959, the House of Dior once again staged a show at Blenheim Palace in aid of the British Red Cross, with Princess Margaret as the guest of honour. This time, the designer-in-chief was the young Yves Saint Laurent, and the Dior label continued to show a separate London collection under a succession of talented designers until 1976.

OPPOSITE Dior enjoyed fantastic editorial coverage from American fashion magazines, including this 1956 shot of famous model Dovima posing in a Dior gown, surrounded by bolts of fabric, under the elevated railway in New York.

RIGHT Determined to keep up momentum after his New Look, Christian Dior was tireless in finding the finest fabrics for his later collections.

A NEW SILHOUETTE

In 1951, Christian Dior started to move away from his New Look silhouette with the launch of what he called the "Natural" line. Gone were the exaggeratedly padded hips and wide, stiffened skits, to be replaced instead by a focus on the oval. "Oval of the face, oval of the bust, oval of the hips: these three superimposed ovals ... follow the *natural* curves of the female body," he explained. The biggest departure was that skirts and suits for daywear now tapered gently towards the hem in a slim column and waists were no longer cinched tightly but tailored into a more natural shape. Jackets had lost the stiff corseting and Edwardian-style peplum to hang more loosely as far as the hip. Feminine curves were still gently accentuated but the overall effect was far less extreme and, for many women, infinitely more wearable. The only dresses where Dior continued to let himself exhibit theatrics were in his evening wear collection, where his love of embellishment, glorious fabrics and grand flourishes was indulged.

The "Natural" line collection was succeeded by the "Long" line, the favourite of all Dior's collections, which

RIGHT In 1951, Dior introduced his "Natural" line collection. Corseted waists and extravagantly padded hips were replaced with designs that gave a more natural shape, using a cutaway short jacket and longer-length skirt.

RIGHT This 1951 dress, with its low décolletage and belted waist, shows that even within his more natural silhouette, Dior still accentuated feminine curves in his designs.

boasted an even lengthier silhouette: skirts dropped to below the calf and his iconic peplum jacket was shortened so that the eye was drawn down a great length of skirt, emphasizing the slenderness of the woman's figure. The designer explained that his previous tricks to deceive the eye to create an artificial figure of womanhood were "out of date. Fashion is all about what is natural and sincere".

Dior continued to focus on a more natural celebration of womanly curves, playing with skirt lengths, presenting a jacket line unbroken at the waist and generally sculpting his designs to make women appear slimmer and more elongated than ever before. His always demure colour palette now veered more towards black than the lighter tones he had favoured previously. Once again, only in his evening wear did he give free rein to his expressionism, creating richly embroidered gowns accessorized by wonderful statement jewellery.

Dior's love of flowers was well known, and he labelled his Spring/Summer 1953 collection the "Tulip" line, following it a year later with the "Lily of the Valley" line, after his

RIGHT This "paletot" was loose and full under the arms and fell to the hip, heralding a new silhouette. The design was described by *Vogue* as "a box coat with Chinese ancestry".

OPPOSITE This 1951 tulle ball dress, with glass beads and sequins and a large velvet bow detail across the bust, illustrates Dior's love of embellishment.

RIGHT Dior had a love of exotic, decadent fabrics, as shown in this outfit of a black-and-gold Persian-style lamé cocktail dress worn under a matching coat lined with black seal fur.

OPPOSITE Dior's childhood obsession with flowers and the garden led to a long-lasting love of floral fabrics and embellishments. This bold printed leaf and bird design is draped by the designer in an approximation of the gown it will become.

ABOVE These three-piece outfits made up of blouse, wool-crepe sweater and pleated skirt with kid gloves and brimless straw bonnets to match are a perfect example of Dior's 1952 "Long" line, with its lengthened and softened silhouette.

ABOVE This stunning ice-blue beaded satin ball gown, shown in *Vogue* in 1952, is classic Dior: tiny waist, curved hips and intricately beaded floral pattern, joined by a matching stole and gloves.

lucky flower. Vivid blues, pinks and purples brought to mind a carpet of mountain flowers and the prints and embroidery he used in the collection all had a floral theme inspired by gardens and orchards.

Throughout his final years, Dior created clothes that would become iconic designs. His mid-fifties collections of the "H", "A", and "Y" lines interpreted the female form in the shapes of these letters, with "A line" becoming common

ABOVE During the 1950s, Dior continued to create the grandest and most romantic of ball gowns, such as this delicately beaded pale pink strapless gown and organdie coat.

parlance in fashion. As the decade moved on, the brand's silhouettes became rounder and softer, impeccably structured as always yet somehow freer. Dior's final collection was Autumn/Winter 1957/58, in which he revealed his two extremes as a designer more than ever before: elegant day dresses and suits were shorter than in previous years and far less fitted; in contrast, his evening wear was extremely structured, with corseted torsos and billowing skirts. As

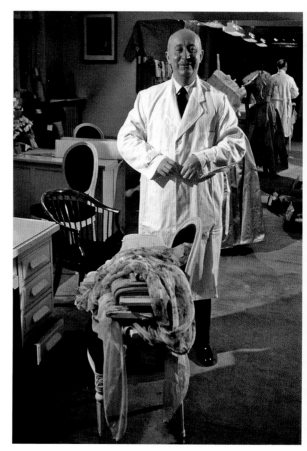

RIGHT During the 10 years that Dior headed his own couture house, he was incredibly involved in every aspect of designing and making the seasonal collections, inspecting garments at every stage of production.

American *Vogue* editor Jessica Daves wrote: "throughout, there is the unflagging professional perfection that explains … the continuing Dior eminence". No one could have foreseen that this would be the immensely talented designer's final collection, his career cut cruelly short by his sudden death from a heart attack while on holiday in Italy on 24 October 1957.

RIGHT This black suit is from Dior's "H" line, shown in Autumn/Winter 1954/55, which he described as focusing on a "lengthening and shrinking of the bust". The waist is skimmed rather than tightly drawn in and the jacket falls straight from sloped shoulders to the hips giving an overall longer, slimmer shape.

HISTORICAL INFLUENCES

The influence of historical fashion on Dior's – and subsequent designers' – collections is hugely important, and his final evening wear collection drew particular inspiration from famous eighteenth-century beauties, including Marie Antoinette and Madame de Pompadour. A preoccupation with this period is obvious from his New Look, with its exaggerated, padded hips and waists tightly corseted in. The fabrics Dior favoured were deeply evocative of the eighteenth century and sumptuous silks and velvets with intricate embroidery became a mainstay of his evening wear collections. The Belle Époque, so reminiscent of Dior's mother, also held sway over the designer, with its fluid lines and the way women were romanticized, something Dior continued to do throughout his career. The designers who succeeded Christian Dior also felt this historical influence deeply, and it surfaced in both traditional and innovative

BELOW RIGHT For Spring/Summer 1955, the "A" line silhouette is modelled at Dior's Paris showroom in front of fashion press, including Carmel Snow of *Harper's Bazaar*, who first coined the term "New Look", and Alexander Liberman of American *Vogue*.

OPPOSITE Dior's "A" line silhouette has became a fashion classic. Similar to the "H" line, the cross of the "A" plays on the waist and the skirt is more flared and often pleated. Narrow shoulders complete the shape.

ways in the haute couture collections of John Galliano, Raf Simons and Maria Grazia Chiuri in particular.

To this day, Dior remains a design house with a strong grounding in what has come before. The designers who came after Christian Dior have not only honoured his nostalgia for the styles of previous centuries but also continued to create designs that reinterpret and acknowledge the importance of his own contribution to fashion history: the New Look.

ABOVE This 1956 tweed coat and sack dress ensemble showed Dior had moved towards a more relaxed silhouette. While starkly different from his original sharply drawn New Look, these outfits were nevertheless extremely elegant and always perfectly accessorized.

ABOVE In the year before his untimely death, Dior had become so popular that his salon was tightly packed each time a new haute couture collection was shown.

OPPOSITE Dior's final collection based around the shape of a letter was the "Y line" shown in Autumn/Winter 1955–56. It showed a higher bust and new way of setting armholes combined with loose-fitting coats and jackets and long, slim skirts.

Hollywood
& Socialites

DIOR
AND
HOLLYWOOD

Christian Dior's reputation as the designer of the
moment spread quickly.

Although his profile was high, Christian Dior was not only
a talented designer but also a savvy businessman, and he
soon realized the necessity of bringing his designs to a wider
audience outside the rarefied atmosphere of haute couture
Paris, wider even than that which he had reached already
with licensing deals.

Of course, the designer needed his fabulous haute couture
dresses to inspire ordinary women to lust after his ready-to-
wear outfits, and few popularized the designer more than
the Hollywood sirens of the silver screen. Many leading
ladies already revered Christian Dior for his glamorous and
feminine designs, so it was inevitable that he would go on to
create dresses for their films. One such muse was Marlene
Dietrich, with whom Dior already had a close friendship.
When offered the role in Alfred Hitchcock's 1950 film *Stage*

OPPOSITE Dior designed the dresses for Marlene
Dietrich in the 1950 film *Stage Fright* after the actress
told director Alfred Hitchcock, "No Dior, No Dietrich!"

RIGHT German actress Marlene Dietrich wearing a Dior outfit in the 1951 film *No Highway in the Sky*.

Fright, the actress allegedly told the director: "No Dior, no Dietrich!" Dior went on to create all the dresses she wore in that film and future productions, including *No Highway in the Sky* in 1951. Other stars who were fans of the designer included Ava Gardner, for whom he designed all costumes for the 1957 film *The Little Hut*, and Olivia de Havilland, who wore a Dior wedding dress in the 1956 film *The Ambassador's Daughter*. Grace Kelly chose a Dior gown to announce her engagement in 1956, and the roll call of big-name actresses continued with Marilyn Monroe, Ingrid Bergman, Sophia Loren (who reputedly spent hours looking at dress samples, cigarette in hand) and Rita Hayworth, who wore Dior to the premiere of *Gilda*. Elizabeth Taylor was a long-time fan of the designer both before and after his death, remaining a loyal customer of the House of Dior; in 1961, she accepted her Best Actress Academy Award wearing a Dior dress and even commissioned matching outfits for herself and her young daughter, Liza.

RIGHT Dior dressed many Hollywood actresses on and off screen. Here, he fits Jane Russell in 1954 with a "Mazette" ensemble from his "H" line, comprising a wool crepe dress and mink fur collar.

RIGHT Grace Kelly appeared in one of Dior's tailored, elegant gowns when she announced her engagement to Prince Rainier of Monaco in 1956.

OPPOSITE Olivia de Havilland is shown here with Dior when she wore one of his wedding dresses for *The Ambassador's Daughter* in 1956.

Dior dresses have since regularly appeared on the red carpet. Nicole Kidman wore a fitted bespoke gown, designed by the newly appointed John Galliano, in a striking and controversial chartreuse to the 1997 Oscars. Galliano later commented, "Nicole looked like a goddess and showed the world she believed in me." To accept her 2013 Best Actress Oscar, Jennifer Lawrence wore a romantic pale pink and white floral-embossed silk Dior ball gown designed by Raf Simons, which she famously tripped over as she walked up to

ABOVE When she
married in 1955,
prima ballerina
Margot Fonteyn wore
a knee-length silk
taffeta Dior wedding
gown with a crossover
neckline, an "H"-line
lengthened and
tailored waist, three-
quarter sleeves and a
full skirt.

the stage. These are the most exquisite of all haute couture
gowns, and they are laboured over for days – or 1,000 hours
in the case of the raffia-embroidered dress, designed by
Maria Grazia Chiuri to look like a "little French garden",
that Nicole Kidman wore to the 2017 Cannes Film Festival.
And they come with a hefty price tag: Charlize Theron's
couture gown for the 2013 Oscars cost $100,000.

The glamour Hollywood has imparted to the Christian
Dior label since the 1950s has filtered down through the
brand to today's ready-to-wear, perfume, cosmetics and
accessories, making it one of the world's most successful
luxury brands. This is thanks in no small part to the choice
of beautiful, elegant actresses, all of whom epitomize the
Dior woman, to represent the label. These have included
Jennifer Lawrence, who appeared in a campaign for the

RIGHT Sophia Loren was a loyal customer who spent hours looking at dress samples and choosing shoes and accessories at Dior's Paris salon.

BELOW RIGHT To accept her 1961 Academy Award for *Butterfield 8*, Elizabeth Taylor wore a sleeveless Dior gown by Marc Bohan with a pale lemon silk bodice and flared white skirt with embroidered flowers and silk sash waist embellished with a red rose.

"Miss Dior" handbag; Marion Cotillard, who became
the face of the brand in 2009; Charlize Theron, who was
signed by John Galliano in 2003 and is the face of the *J'adore*
fragrance; and Natalie Portman, who represents the label's
beauty and fragrance line and who starred in the short
advertising film *La Vie en Rose*, directed by Sofia Coppola.

OPPOSITE LEFT
Charlize Theron wore a
striking midnight-blue
strapless fishtail gown by
John Galliano for Dior to
the 2005 Golden Globes.

OPPOSITE RIGHT
Marion Cotillard, one of
the faces of Dior, wore a
stunning sequinned blue
gown with full net skirt,
cinched at the waist by
a patent belt, to the 81st
Academy Awards in 2009.

RIGHT Natalie Portman,
who represents Dior
fragrance and cosmetics,
wore this Dior haute
couture red with black
polka dots strapless silk
organza gown to the 84th
Academy Awards in 2012.

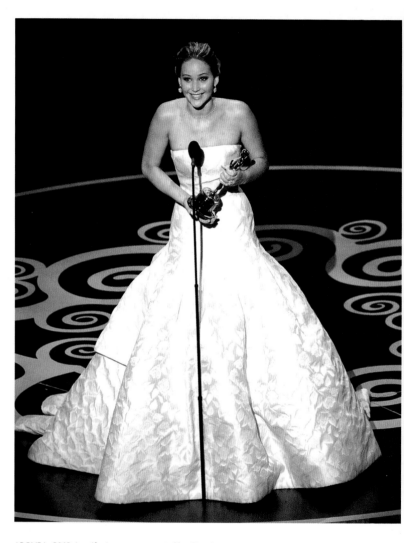

ABOVE In 2013, Jennifer Lawrence accepted her Best Actress
award for *Silver Linings Playbook* wearing a pale pink and white
floral-embossed silk Dior ball gown designed by Raf Simons, which
she famously tripped over as she walked up to the stage.

ROYALTY AND DEBUTANTES

At age 21, Dior spent several months in London and later
wrote in his autobiography: "There is no country in the
world besides my own ... I like so much." Of dressing English
women, he said: "I find them amongst the most beautiful and
distinguished in the world. When an English woman is pretty
she is prettier than a woman of any other nationality."

LEFT Princess
Margaret sat for
society photographer
Cecil Beaton for her
official twenty-first
birthday portrait in
July 1951, wearing
an exquisite off-
the-shoulder white
Dior gown featuring
draped tulle, intricate
embroidery, sequins
and pearls.

RIGHT The Duchess of Windsor, who lived in Paris, was well known for her impeccable dress sense. This 1951 photograph of the exiled royal, wearing a Dior ball gown with beaded flowers, appeared in American *Vogue* magazine.

OPPOSITE Christian Dior had admired Josephine Baker for years, watching her perform at the Folies Bergère long before he became a fashion designer. The entertainer wore his gowns on stage for her 1951 tour of the United States.

Dior's first showing in London was his second collection in the autumn of 1947. It was a sumptuous affair at the Savoy hotel and the next morning, Dior was invited to give a private showing to the then-Queen; Princess Margaret; Marina, Duchess of Kent; and the Duchess' sister Princess Olga of Yugoslavia. A confirmed royalist, Dior noted the "elegance" and "graciousness" of the Queen, but it was Princess Margaret who captured the very essence of the beautiful English rose. He described her as "a real fairytale princess, delicate, graceful, exquisite … [who] knew exactly the sort of fashions that suited her fragile height and Titania-like figure". The admiration was mutual – the young princess had a keen interest in fashion and the finely tailored, hourglass-shaped designs of the New Look were perfectly suited to her.

Princess Margaret was the most glamorous and lovely of the young royals, and in July 1951 she sat for society photographer Cecil Beaton for her official 21st birthday

portrait wearing an exquisite off-the-shoulder white Dior gown featuring draped tulle, intricate embroidery, sequins and pearls. The aesthetic was pure New Look, with a tiny waist and extravagantly full skirt. The princess became a loyal client of the House of Dior, as did other members of the British aristocracy. The author Nancy Mitford, who lived in Paris, was smitten by the New Look collection and purchased the black "Daisy" suit, which she described as: "Simply, to my mind, perfect."

Dior dresses were also sought after among debutantes, as they were required to wear new outfits for every social occasion in the busy coming-out season, and the "debs" were keen to make an impression by wearing the latest fashions. In 1953, a debutante fashion show was organized in aid of the NSPCC (the National Society for the Prevention of Cruelty to Children) at the Berkeley hotel. The final piece of the collection, the wedding dress, was an exquisite creation made from fine muslin and embroidered with white flowers and delicate metal leaves. It was later presented to a delighted Jane Stoddart, a 19-year-old bride with the classic hourglass figure of the Dior woman, who wore the dress to her London wedding.

Charity fashion shows remained an excellent way of publicizing Dior's designs in Britain, where the press had a greedy appetite for the glamorous upper classes. In 1954, the Duchess of Marlborough organized a show in aid of the British Red Cross at Blenheim Palace with Princess Margaret as the guest of honour.

Thirteen carefully selected models paraded a selection of Dior's new "H" line Autumn/Winter 1954 collection in front of almost two thousand guests. It was one of the few fashion presentations that Dior attended as a guest. As a tribute, he was made an honorary member of the British Red Cross and presented with a diploma by Princess Margaret. After the show, he was mobbed by a crowd of Red Cross nurses clamouring for autographs. In his autobiography, Dior wrote glowingly of his impression of the grand Blenheim Palace, although admitted to feeling slightly awkward showing French fashion among tapestries celebrating the defeat of the French, in the home built for the Duke of Marlborough: "At any moment I expected his indignant ghost to join the line of mannequins!"

A more recent member of the British royal family who favoured the brand, as avidly followed by the press as the young Princess Margaret, was Princess Diana. She often chose elegant suits from the fashion house and, in 1995, she

OPPOSITE TOP
Dior was very popular among the British upper classes, and in 1953, a debutante fashion show was organized for the NSPCC at The Berkeley hotel.

OPPOSITE BELOW
Charity fashion shows were an excellent way to publicize Dior designs, especially with royals like Princess Margaret present. This 1954 Blenheim Palace show in aid of the British Red Cross saw the models parade among tapestries celebrating Marlborough's defeat of the French, a juxtaposition Dior found ironic.

had the iconic "Lady Dior" handbag named for her. But it was Diana's choice of John Galliano's first-ever creation for Dior that stole the limelight: a controversial slip-like peacock-blue silk dress with lace detailing that the princess wore to the Met Ball in New York in 1996. Rumour has it she almost didn't wear the dress, worrying that the then-14-year-old Prince William would be shocked to see his mother wear something so revealing.

Plenty of other royals have chosen Dior designs too, the restrained elegance of the label perfectly suiting diplomatic and state occasions. Princess Charlene of Monaco frequently chooses Dior gowns for balls and galas as well as simple shift dresses or suits for other public occasions. Queen Rania of Jordan, renowned for her effortless sense of style, is another fan, and Queen Mathilde of Belgium often appears in the brand's timeless suits, so redolent of the 1950s. The younger generation – including fashion model and royal Lady Amelia Windsor, a firm fixture on the Dior front row – aren't afraid to showcase some of the label's more risqué designs including the iconic white-with-black-polka-dots transparent dress, complete with visible branded Dior underwear, from the Spring/Summer 2018 show. As proof that Dior is a failsafe label for new royals hoping to strike the stately tone so associated with the British monarchy, Meghan Markle, now the Duchess of Sussex, turned to the brand as she joined the royal family. For the RAF centenary service at Westminster Abbey, she chose a perfectly tailored Maria Grazia Chiuri black satin dress with a boat neck, nipped-in waist and flared skirt that felt like a modern take on the iconic dresses of Christian Dior's groundbreaking New Look collection.

OPPOSITE In 1996, Princess Diana wore John Galliano's first-ever creation for Dior to the Met Ball in New York. The controversially slip-like peacock-blue silk dress with lace detailing caused outrage among some commentators, who felt it was too provocative for a member of the royal family.

Dior Without Dior

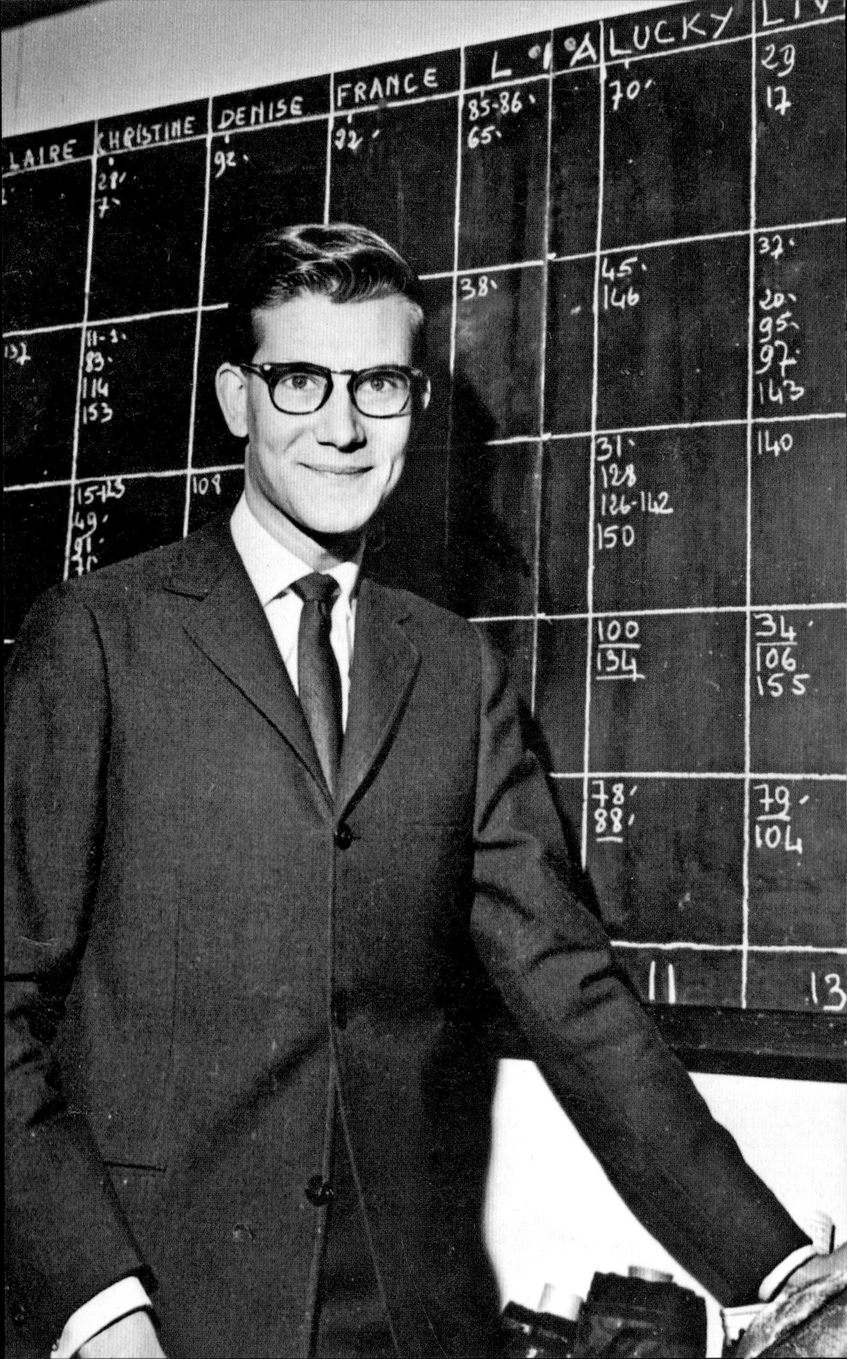

CHRISTINE
DENISE
FRANCE
LUCKY

MAINTAINING DIOR'S LEGACY

Christian Dior died after heading his eponymous house for just 10 years but his legacy is such that the designers who have succeeded him have remained true to the original tenets of the New Look: masterful cut and tailoring, celebration of the female form, exotic and historical influences, and theatrical presentation.

YVES SAINT LAURENT 1957–1960

Algerian-born Yves Saint Laurent showed a prodigious talent for fashion design even as a student in Paris, where he won several prestigious prizes at the age of just 18. French *Vogue* editor Michel de Brunhoff took the young designer under his wing, immensely impressed when Saint Laurent showed him fashion sketches that bore close similarities to ones drawn by Dior himself featuring the new "A" line silhouette. An introduction was made in 1955, and Dior immediately hired the younger man. Saint Laurent soon started submitting designs for the haute couture collections, and by the mid-1950s, he had become invaluable to Dior.

OPPOSITE Yves Saint Laurent poses by the model schedule in the atelier of the House of Dior, 1958.

RIGHT For his Dior debut, Yves Saint Laurent introduced the "Trapeze" line – a beautifully elegant collection dedicated to the late designer, which received rave reviews.

OPPOSITE A year after Dior's untimely death, Yves Saint Laurent followed in his footsteps by taking his collection to Britain for a second charity fashion show in aid of the Red Cross at Blenheim Palace. Princess Margaret presented the designer with a Red Cross Badge of Honour, as she had done for Christian Dior.

In August 1957, Dior met with Saint Laurent's mother to tell her that he had chosen her son to succeed him as head designer. Given Dior's relatively young age, the remark was mystifying, and yet fate intervened. Later that year, at just 21 years old, Yves Saint Laurent found himself head of the famous couture house.

Saint Laurent's first collection for Dior, which was called the "Trapeze" line and dedicated to the late designer, was a huge success. The new head designer built on Dior's original "A" line silhouette to present a collection that was beautifully balanced, with an elegant symmetry between wide, scooped necklines and billowing, full skirts. The relief among

OPPOSITE Yves Saint Laurent puts the finishing touches on an evening gown for his Spring/Summer 1959 collection.

RIGHT Yves Saint Laurent experimented with modern fashions, including the hobble skirt shown here as part of this blue satin evening gown for his Autumn/Winter 1959/60 collection.

ABOVE Towards the end of his short tenure at Dior, Yves Saint Laurent looked to beatniks and other youth culture for inspiration, which was not well received by those who respected the traditional elegance of Dior.

the fashion press was palpable, with *The New York Times* commenting: "Rarely does a hoped-for miracle come off just on time … today's magnificent collection has made a French national hero of Dior's successor, 22-year-old Yves Saint Laurent, and comfortably assures the future of the house that Dior built."

However, Saint Laurent's tenure was short-lived, as he resisted the slow, gentle fluctuations in style and hemline that was expected of a genteel couture house such as Dior.

Clients and press alike were scathing of his revolutionary new designs, including hobble skirts and beatnik-influenced pieces. In retrospect, Saint Laurent's creations were prescient, but he spoke to the future, not the present. By taking inspiration from youth culture and reflecting it in haute couture, he inevitably alienated himself from the respectability of the Dior brand. An immensely exciting and talented designer, he went on to achieve enormous success, but unfortunately Dior was not the right house in which to showcase his fashion vision. When the designer was called up for military service in 1960, he was replaced by Marc Bohan.

MARC BOHAN 1961–1989

The House of Dior could not have found a designer more different to Yves Saint Laurent than Marc Bohan. Older by a decade and far more experienced in the world of haute

BELOW Marc Bohan arriving in New York in 1955 with 10 Dior models. Little did he suspect that five years later, he would be head of the haute couture house.

couture, Bohan was deeply respectful of its traditions. The designer was no stranger to the label either. In 1957, having admired Bohan's work at houses such as Molyneux and Jean Patou, Dior asked him to head up the brand's New York operation. Dior died before he could appoint Bohan to this role and, with tension brewing between Bohan and Yves Saint Laurent, the new head designer was reluctant to honour the offer. Bohan was well respected by other partners at Dior, so instead moved to Dior London and when the volatile Saint Laurent was drafted for military service, he was replaced by the steadfast Bohan. The decision was an astute one. Clients and buyers were troubled by Saint Laurent's radical new fashion direction – ironically, given the

furore caused by Dior's original New Look – because Dior was now seen as a timeless label to trust for style classics.

Bohan spent 29 years as head of Dior, and in that time, the fashion and haute couture industries changed unrecognizably. Not only did fashions vary wildly through the 1960s and 1970s, but also the practice of selling original Paris designs to department stores for reproduction on a large scale was replaced by ready-to-wear. These additional

collections, targeted at a wider buying public and imbued
with all the cachet of the designer label, would become a
major source of revenue for couture houses. Ready-to-wear
collections were shown two weeks before the grandeur
of haute couture; by the 1970s, the number of designers
presenting these shows became so high that, in 1973,
the regulatory Chambre Syndicale du Prêt-à-Porter des
Couturiers et des Créateurs de Mode (soon to be known as

OPPOSITE LEFT
This simple, slim-belted floral dress with neck-bow detail, perfectly accessorized with a wide hat, long gloves and pointed heels, is typical of the wearable and elegant outfits that gained Bohan such a loyal clientele.

OPPOSITE RIGHT
A 1963 lilac, belted drop-waisted top with skirt and matching hat in fashionable tweed combines the elegance of Dior with the fashions of the 1960s.

RIGHT Bohan had a particular talent for designing evening wear, such as this exotically beaded, sleeveless Byzantine-inspired dress from the late 1960s.

Paris Fashion Week) was founded. It was Yves Saint Laurent
who launched one of the first ready-to-wear collections with
his own Rive Gauche boutique, but Bohan followed soon
after, launching Dior's "Miss Dior" line in 1967. Other
changes followed, with the launch of "Baby Dior" in 1967
and "Dior Homme" menswear in 1970. Bohan also oversaw
the expansion of Dior's fragrance business. In 1969, Dior
presented its first complete line of cosmetics and the brand

had at last achieved Christian Dior's goal to provide for
every part of a woman's appearance.

Marc Bohan never wavered from the foundations of
Dior's design ethos. His clothes were always masterfully
cut with a sculptured precision in their silhouette, and
he was modern without being flashy. His first collection
in 1961, titled the "Slim Look", took the 1920s influence
that so many designers were exhibiting that season but

ABOVE A 1975 shot
of Jerry Hall wearing
a blue one-shouldered
satin column dress
with luxurious feather
trim shows Bohan's
tailored glamour at
its best.

gave it a fresh, young aesthetic, streamlined and simple
and most importantly, infinitely wearable. *Women's Wear
Daily* commented: "Bohan has done the impossible: he
is a big commercial success and respected by the fashion
intellectuals".

Bohan may not have had the fashion genius of Yves Saint
Laurent, or even of the later John Galliano, but he provided

RIGHT Like Yves Saint Laurent before him and Raf Simons after, Bohan experimented with androgynous styles, and in the 1980s, presented a wide-shouldered long tuxedo jacket offset with killer heels and an accent of red.

FAR RIGHT
Marc Bohan oversaw the launch of the label's first menswear line, "Dior Homme", in 1970.

a timeless elegance essential to the longevity of a house like Dior. He took the fashions of the day and elevated them to haute couture. His particular talent for designing evening wear saw the creation of stunningly embellished gowns in exotic fabrics, of which Dior himself would have been proud. But Bohan's most formidable skill, which enabled him to maintain the largest number of haute couture clients

of any house in Paris, lay in pleasing his female customers. "Don't forget the woman" was his motto, and many devoted customers flocked to the new designer. Elizabeth Taylor bought 12 dresses from his debut collection and Jacqueline Kennedy Onassis, Sophia Loren and Princess Grace of Monaco all turned regularly to Dior for Bohan's effortless sense of style.

Bohan left Dior in 1989 first to design for Norman Hartnell, and later to concentrate on designing under his own name.

GIANFRANCO FERRÉ 1989–1996

In 1984, Dior was bought by Bernard Arnault, the French financier who would go on to become the wealthy and influential chairman of LVMH[1], the world's largest luxury goods company. Gianfranco Ferré was the first designer to be appointed by Arnault as he sought to restore the fortunes and boost the international reputation of the Dior label.

RIGHT Ferré received a De D'Or award for his first collection, which featured immaculately tailored suits worn with top hats and was inspired by the Ascot finery of Cecil Beaton's costumes from the 1964 film *My Fair Lady*.

OPPOSITE For his 1989 debut collection, Ferré stayed true to the New Look aesthetic, creating ball gowns in sumptuous fabrics with florals printed or embroidered onto the fabric with added embellishments and cascading flowers.

1 In 1984, Moët Hennessy – Louis Vuitton SE (LVMH), the luxury goods group headed by French billionaire Bernard Arnault, bought the Boussac company, then about to go bankrupt, giving the company the fashion label which quickly became the cornerstone of its empire. In 2017, LVMH finally bought the 25.9% of Dior that it did not own, consolidating the brand.

LEFT Like Dior himself, Ferré loved glamour, epitomized by this long, gold sheath dress made from velvet panne with a taffeta silk cape from his Autumn/Winter 1993/94 haute couture collection.

Ferré was a somewhat controversial choice. He was an Italian (at a time when the rivalry between French and Italian fashion was at an all-time high) with a background in ready-to-wear, not haute couture. Nevertheless, Ferré was a natural fit for the house. Trained as an architect (he became widely known as "the architect of fashion"), a career Dior himself once considered, Ferré understood the importance of a garment's underlying structure and form and shared much of Dior's aesthetic. Both men idolized their stylish mothers, celebrated the feminine and found inspiration in travel – Ferré spent three years studying in India in the early 1970s and was heavily influenced by the colours and traditions he found there. But perhaps the most important similarity was a love of glamour, theatre and overtly stylized silhouettes rich with embellishment and decoration. These all came easily to Ferré, who had produced a collection inspired by *La Dolce Vita* for his own label in the 1980s.

BELOW Before the new collections, Ferré would spend three days locked in the Dior salon going through thousands of items, including shoes, jewellery, gloves, scarves and hats, to choose the perfect accessories for each outfit.

Gianfranco Ferré's experience in ready-to-wear was important too. Haute couture was still the glamorous face of Dior, but relatively few women could afford the hefty price tags these outfits carried. The theatricality of the Paris shows became a marketing tool, while ready-to-wear, menswear and diffusion lines into accessories, fragrance and cosmetics provided the financial ballast. Ferré, with his background in jewellery design, ready-to-wear, menswear and accessories for his own label was well placed to steer Dior though this shift in the fashion industry.

Ferré's first collection for Dior was called "Ascot-Cecil Beaton", and was inspired by the costumes created by Beaton for the 1964 film *My Fair Lady*. By combining Dior's love of Edwardian style with the Ascot finery of Beaton's film, Ferré found a masculine foil to the femininity of decorative Edwardian dresses. He described his look as juxtaposing "austere masculine fabrics – tweed, barathea, flannel, Prince of Wales check – with exquisitely feminine white blouses in silk, voile and organza". Models wore suits and matching top hats in Dior's beloved muted grey, accessorized with an enormous bow that became Ferré's trademark. Evening wear was as sumptuous as ever, with floor-length dresses made from silk faille, duchesse satin and organza with embroidered pearls and jewels. And as a tribute to Dior's love of flowers, roses, lilies of the valley and country flowers were printed onto fabrics, pinned corsage-style or cascaded extravagantly from ballgowns. The clothes were as perfectly constructed as Dior himself would have demanded. American *Vogue* summed up Ferré's debut as "a matter of Dior discipline and Ferré flourish". The designer was awarded the prestigious Dé D'Or (Golden Thimble) for his first collection.

During his seven-year tenure at Dior, Ferré stayed

OPPOSITE Beautifully tailored outfits were given Ferré's trademark oversized flourishes, seen here in the oversized sleeves, long gloves and large matching hat from his Autumn/ Winter 1995 haute couture show.

ABOVE Like Dior himself, Ferré loved the theatre of fashion and was more than happy to take the applause.

true to the New Look aesthetic, with its curvaceous silhouette, immaculate structure and craftsmanship and use of imaginative textiles and fabrics. The strong lines of his creations, referencing the tightly cinched waist and exaggeratedly curved skirts, were as sculptural as Dior's original designs. Ferré freely acknowledged how much Dior's revolutionary New Look underpinned his own collections, commenting: "I don't want to live with a ghost, but I respect the couture tradition." Ferré did leave his own mark on the house with oversized bows and equally outsized cuffs and lapels, influences from the East and exaggerated elements in shoulders, flared sleeves and billowing skirts. Looking back on his collections, there is a strong sense of late-1980s and early-1990s fashion, not an era readily compared to the elegance of the 1950s. It is testament to Ferré's skill as a designer that he managed to create modern designs that still retained an echo of Dior's original New Look. Ferré left Dior in 1996 to focus on his own label.

JOHN GALLIANO 1996–2011

Almost exactly 50 years after Christian Dior presented his groundbreaking New Look, a similar visionary took over the reins at the House of Dior: British designer John Galliano, whose first haute couture collection hit the catwalks in January 1997. Galliano had already proved his credentials at Givenchy – where, in 1995, he became the first British designer to lead a French couture house since the end of World War II – before being moved to Dior in 1996 by LVMH owner Bernard Arnault.

The move could not have been more apt. Galliano had long revered the designs of Dior and shared many of the same visions. Both men had travelled widely, were particularly influenced by exotic cities and cultures and had

BELOW In 1996, Galliano took over at Dior, immediately stamping his personality on the label by designing flamboyantly feminine gowns inspired by Christian Dior's own love of the exaggerated female form.

a love of historical romanticism. The latter was abundantly
clear in Galliano's lauded Central St Martin's graduate
show, which was titled "Les Incroyables" and was inspired
by the flamboyant eighteenth-century dandies of the French
Revolution. Galliano also shared Dior's obsession with the
exaggerated female form, and his masterful skill in creating
almost architecturally structured clothes echoed that of the
legendary designer.

On his appointment, Galliano declared, "It is the greatest house in the world. To be given the reins of the house is something I would never have believed could happen." In homage to Christian Dior's first show, Galliano staged his debut haute couture collection for the label at the Grand Hotel in Paris, where a larger-than-life version of Dior's original salon had been built, complete with dove-grey drapery and a grand central staircase. The show itself harked back to the French designer's love of the Belle Époque, a halcyon time epitomized by Dior's mother's style and romanticized in his future collections, juxtaposed with Galliano's fascination with the Maasai people. Shapes from the New Look, including the iconic "Bar" line with its tiny waist and flared hips, were used by Galliano, but softened and shortened. The "S" line silhouette was featured frequently, presented in vibrant colours. Like Dior, Galliano relied heavily on accessories to create a look, and that first show featured dramatic Maasai-inspired breastplates, bracelets and plate-collars. It was a forceful arrival that set the stage for the next 15 years.

John Galliano had remarkable skill in blending East and West: his first ready-to-wear collection, nicknamed "Dior Pin-ups", was inspired by Hollywood icons such as Marilyn Monroe and Brigitte Bardot as well as Chinese pin-up models from the 1930s. Future shows featured Raj-inspired Mata Hari evening dresses and imagined a meeting between Wallis Simpson and Pocahontas. His love of theatre meant that his haute couture shows – complete with cutting-edge set design and models made into imaginary characters – were more akin to watching a performance than a fashion show.

Throughout his time at Dior, Galliano pushed the boundaries of fashion design. While remaining true to

OPPOSITE Like Dior, Galliano was inspired by different cultures, and his Autumn/Winter 2001/02 collection took inspiration from Tibet.

the label's Edwardian aesthetic, his collections variously introduced sportswear, Russian and Chinese military uniforms, nods to Communism, and surrealist, Dali-esque tailoring in which jackets were worn back to front. Female emancipation was a strong theme, with warrior-like models stalking the runway, and his social commentary was most evident in his controversial 2000 haute couture show "Clochards", which was inspired by Paris's homeless population and saw newspaper-printed silk dresses deconstructed and pinned with rags.

There is no doubt that throughout Galliano's tenure at Dior, he created a truly remarkable variety of designs. The British designer never forgot the ethos of Christian Dior himself, always paying incredible attention to detail in the tailoring and embellishment of his own designs, while his eclectic interests and inexhaustible creative energy made him the most flamboyant of designers at the House of Dior. Galliano's time at Dior came to an abrupt end in 2011 when he was fired after accusations emerged that he had twice made anti-semitic and racist remarks to patrons of a Paris bar. Blaming his drug and alcohol addictions, he was later charged and fined 6,000 Euros.

BILL GAYTTEN 2011–2012

Bill Gaytten is not a name usually included in the roll call of designers for Dior, as he was only a temporary replacement. However, it is worth acknowledging the job he did holding down the fort after the scandal of John Galliano's departure. Gaytten had worked alongside Galliano for 23 years, first at the designer's own label, then at Givenchy and finally at Dior. His role as studio head was essentially overseeing the creation of the garments, but not their design, so the

OPPOSITE For the 60th anniversary of Dior, Galliano created a tribute collection called "The Artists' Ball", designing extravagant dresses for it, such as this red ball gown, worn by Linda Evangelista, with a curvaceous silhouette and beaded, floral embellishments.

appointment was a rude awakening for the reserved Gaytten, who was more used to being behind the scenes than thrust into the limelight. He took over just four days before the Autumn/Winter 2011 ready-to-wear collection was due to hit the catwalk, but stewarded Galliano's final collection and stayed on to design two haute couture and two ready-to-wear collections.

Gaytten was not treated particularly well by the fashion press, which was clamouring for a high-profile design talent to be appointed as creative director. Nevertheless, he stuck close to the fundamental tenets of the Dior brand, presenting collections based on the New Look and Galliano-style exaggerated silhouettes that were unimpeachable in their design technique. Gaytten's colour palette was restrained and his designs cautious, but he provided a much-needed steadying hand as the repercussions of Galliano's antisemitic outbursts and the revelations of his drink and drug addictions rocked the reputation of the House of Dior.

RAF SIMONS 2012–2015

During the year that Bill Gaytten headed Dior, there was much speculation as to who would take over from John Galliano as creative director, with names like Marc Jacobs and Phoebe Philo in the mix. So different from the theatrical Galliano, Belgian-born designer Raf Simons was not immediately hyped as a contender, although he had a background in industrial design and had generated a great deal of interest since his arrival on the fashion scene. He started his career as a furniture designer and, rather like Dior himself, was fascinated by contemporary art. In 1990, Simons was impressed by a fashion show by fellow Belgian Martin Margiela, an eccentric designer who deconstructed

OPPOSITE In his debut collection, which became the focus of the documentary *Dior et Moi*, Simons recreated the perfect craftsmanship and essential simplicity of Dior's own first collections.

LEFT In a floral dress with the nipped-in waist and full, flared skirt of the New Look, Simons literally deconstructs the legacy of Dior with a cut-out pattern at the waist in place of the classic belt.

OPPOSITE In Simons's Spring/Summer 2015 haute couture collection, named "Moonage Daydream" in homage to David Bowie, he explained his experimental mix as a sensory overload embracing "the romance of the 1950s ... the experimentation of the 1960s and the liberation of the 1970s".

fashion – creating haute couture outfits from unusual sources including second-hand fabrics, discarded canvases, old wigs and silk scarves. The Margiela show, held in a children's playground rather than a grand salon, intrigued Simons. He saw how couture fashion could exist – outside the glamour and parties – and be experienced on an intellectual, emotional plane, much like a work of art.

Simons had no formal training, launching his fashion career with an eponymous menswear label in 1995. His early influences came mainly from youth culture within music, with sources as varied as niche hardcore techno, German electro bands and British rock. His first foray into womenswear came when he was appointed by the German label Jil Sander to create a ready-to-wear line. Sander's utilitarian, minimalist aesthetic had won the brand a core of loyal fans, and her innovative use of fabrics helped define the fashions of the day. But her modern, understated silhouette needed reinvigorating – and Raf Simons did just that, bringing energy to the label. His exhaustive research into precise cuts, use of brightly coloured synthetic materials and his inclination towards ergonomic shapes was revolutionary. Combined with his passion for edgy music and art and his awareness of contemporary culture, Simons's aesthetic spoke to a new generation.

When he joined Dior in 2012, Simons looked back into the Dior archives, like so many of his predecessors. He had used mid-century haute couture silhouettes (albeit reinterpreted in synthetic neons) at Jil Sander, and for his debut collection at Dior, he took the iconic "Bar" jacket and teamed it not with the demure, flared skirt of the 1950s but with narrow trousers. It was an inspired move, a feminine take on masculine dressing, fittingly recalling Yves

ABOVE By teaming
tailored, floral-
embellished jackets
with ultra-mini skirts,
Simons presented
a different take on
Dior's lengthened
silhouette.

Saint Laurent's 1966 revolutionary "Le Smoking" tuxedo for women. Simons deconstructed the legacy of Dior – sometimes literally, as when he presented his take on a floral Dior ball gown but truncated it at the hip to appear more like a bustier top, or when he paired a ball gown featuring a billowing, tulip-like skirt, full of Edwardian romance, with a sportswear-like semi-transparent top.

Raf Simons's first collection for Dior was breathtaking in its both its intellect and execution. Here was an industrially trained designer with a passion for modernity managing to take the classic lines of the Dior archives and reinterpret them in a completely different way. It was a "new look" all over again.

In April 2014, a documentary about the making of the collection, directed and written by Frédéric Tcheng, premiered at the Tribeca Film Festival. *Dior et Moi* revealed as never before the level of artistry and skill that is involved in putting on a haute couture show. From Simons's extensive research of the Dior archives through the design process between the designer and his collaborators to his relationship to the ateliers (some of which had been making the details of Dior's collections by hand for more than 40 years), the documentary was revelatory. Simons comes across as surprisingly humble, sensitive and deeply invested in his work and determined to honour the Dior name while pushing forward into the future. Old techniques, including the time-consuming and expensive method of "imprimé chaîne", where each thread of a fabric is printed before being woven, are revealed to be almost impossible to achieve – and yet Simons is determined to experiment.

Throughout Raf Simons's relatively short time at Dior, his theme of modernizing original designs continued to

ABOVE An essentially humble designer, Simons's passion was for creation rather than the limelight, but he acknowledged the critical acclaim his collections received.

great critical acclaim, and the announcement that he would be departing as creative director after barely three years was surprising. Simons had admitted to frustration at how fast he had to produce collections – six a year, including the two gruelling haute couture shows – and lack of time to be as creative as he would like to be. There was speculation that the Dior brand, with its million-dollar celebrity cosmetics and fragrance contracts and focus on commercial success, made Simons feel alienated from his design ethos. Nevertheless, despite attempts to persuade him to stay, Simons's departure was amicable and he left Dior firmly placed at the forefront of contemporary fashion.

MARIA GRAZIA CHIURI 2016–PRESENT

In July 2016, for the first time, Dior appointed a female creative director, Italian Maria Grazia Chiuri, who had previously worked for Fendi and Valentino. The appointment was a natural one for a fashion house steeped in femininity. From the beginning, the Dior look was all about womanliness, accentuating female curves and creating romantic silhouettes. Dior himself had many formative female influences in his life and Chiuri similarly grew up surrounded and inspired by strong women: her five sisters, grandmother and, most importantly, her mother, a seamstress, who gave her daughter an early love of fashion and appreciation of the craft of creating clothes.

As a woman, Chiuri provides a particular angle on fashion design. She is a working mother and self-proclaimed feminist who appreciates that clothes need to answer many needs – practical, aesthetic and even political. Before her first show, she stated: "I strive to be attentive and to be open to the world and to create fashion that resembles the women of today." In an interview with American *Vogue*, in speaking about women's changing attitudes to fashion in the 1960s, she stressed the importance of how Marc Bohan's designs responded to his client's needs by making dresses shorter and simpler, explaining: "It was not the designer who changed the line, but the woman changed, and the designer understood that the woman was different".

Chiuri's first collection for Dior was ready-to-wear rather than haute couture. In it, she reflected the reality of fashion for all women, not just an elite few. As a result, a wide variety of styles were shown, including sportswear, streetwear, evening wear and casual wear. This melting pot of design included radical pairings such as an intricately beaded skirt

worn with a T-shirt bearing the slogan "We Should All Be Feminists", taken from the title of Chimamanda Ngozi Adichie's 2014 essay. Similarly, Chiuri put the title of Linda Nochlin's 1971 essay "Why Have There Been No Great Women Artists?" on another T-shirt.

Like all new designers to Dior, Chiuri researched the label's archives. But rather than just giving her take on the New Look, she took inspiration from all her predecessors –

RIGHT As a steadfast feminist, Chiuri sent models down the catwalk for her first ready-to-wear collection in T-shirts emblazoned with the slogan "We Should All Be Feminists", the title of the groundbreaking 2014 essay by novelist Chimamanda Ngozi Adichie.

OPPOSITE Chiuri mixed up the transitions of Dior, putting romantic dresses with branded street-style accessories, as worn here by actress Jennifer Lawrence.

reinterpreting their reinterpretations, so to speak. She has variously referenced Yves Saint Laurent, John Galliano and Raf Simons, as well as Hedi Slimane, who headed up Dior Homme from 2012 to 2016. Chiuri likes to play with traditional masculine and feminine roles with a degree of ambiguity and androgyny in many of her designs. Among

all this modernism, however, she still finds influence in historical fashions, which are always an integral part of the Dior brand.

For Chiuri, focusing on wearability is essential to a modern Dior collection; the needs of the client are paramount, with modern tailoring a key element in her designs. But the romanticism that is at the heart of the Dior label is not lost, and she continues to create beautiful evening wear with all the trademark florals and embroidery that embody the Dior fantasy. Her 2019 foray into costume design, for the ballet *Nuit Blanche* at the Teatro Dell'Opera in Rome, is a case in point. For that production, she created ethereal dresses featuring tulle skirts juxtaposed with sportswear-inspired tops printed with Dior's haute couture flowers. Chiuri has reinvented Dior, taking the label from feminine to feminist. The woman who wears the clothes has the power – the designer is simply her translator.

Accessories

DIOR FROM HEAD TO TOE

Christian's Dior's New Look was more than just a revolutionary silhouette – it was a whole ensemble where the hat, shoes, gloves, bag and silk stockings were as important to the look as the dress or suit.

His iconic "Bar" jacket and flared skirt would not have looked the same without the domed straw hat with its instantly recognizable straw brim or the elegant, slim-heeled shoes. The designer regularly examined samples of accessories to pick the perfect ones to complement his outfits.

These accessories were originally made by carefully selected companies to which Dior licensed his name, starting in 1948 with his first deal for the manufacture of hosiery. In an unusual decision for the time, Dior took a percentage of sales rather than simply selling a licence to manufacture under his name. It was a profitable move, and this soon became the norm in the fashion industry. Over the years, the Dior name has been licensed to a wide range of products,

OPPOSITE Christian Dior stands in his showroom in 1955 with samples of design accessories for women, including hats, hat pins, gloves, muffs, lingerie, hosiery, evening bags and jewellery.

including hosiery, corsets, lingerie and furs, with a ready-to-wear fur line launched in 1973 and jewellery, including Dior's first watch, "Black Moon", in 1975.

Initially, these licences were given to well-established companies and designers. This included shoemaker Roger Vivier, who created a line of elegant shoes for Dior in 1953, and glovemaker Dents, who were appointed when Dior opened his London store in 1954. But over the next few decades, the Dior brand chased profit over reputation, overstretched itself and subsequently diluted the image of the couture house. By the 1980s, Dior had licensing agreements with around 200 companies. In an effort to restore the label to its former exclusivity, many of these agreements were allowed to lapse or were bought back. Later collaborations with accessories designers with excellent reputations of their own – such as milliner Stephen Jones, who created fabulous hats for John Galliano's haute couture fashion shows – have also contributed to the success of the Dior brand.

RIGHT Shoes were intricately designed by skilful makers to complement Dior's gowns. This evening shoe by Roger Vivier for Dior has a beautifully sculpted feathered butterfly detail.

RIGHT A black sculpted straw hat from 1951 is an example of Dior's elegant designs, offsetting a pale suit and gloves perfectly.

Bags have arguably become the most important of all Dior accessories, especially in recent years. Under Dior's original tenure, bags, like his clothes, had to be crafted from the finest materials and were painstakingly handmade to fit the sculpted, elegant Dior silhouette for both day and evening wear. In 1954, the designer advised: "You can wear the same suit from morning to dinner but to be really perfectly dressed, you cannot keep the same bag. For morning, it must very simple and for the evening, it must be smaller and, if you wish, a little fancier."

Successive creative heads at Dior have all recognized the importance of providing a complete look for their clientele. With the launch of the Miss Dior ready-to-wear line under Marc Bohan in 1967, accessories became an even more important revenue stream. From there, the explosion in the cachet of the designer labels in the 1980s and 1990s led to the arrival of the so-called "It bag".

In 1995, French President Jacques Chirac's wife Bernadette presented Princess Diana with an elegant, black

ABOVE RIGHT
This elegant pink "Diorever" bag with sequinned butterfly detail shows the same level of craftsmanship as couture gowns.

RIGHT Maria Grazia Chiuri's "Dio(r) evolution" bag has become a cult design.

padded square bag by Dior, then unofficially called the "Chouchou". Diana used the bag so much that it became associated with the much-photographed princess and it was renamed "Princesse" before launching on a larger scale as the "Lady Dior". The association with the most fashionable woman in the world led to Dior selling 200,000 bags over the next two years. Subsequent bags launched by Dior, including John Galliano's 1999 "Saddle" bag – beloved of Carrie Bradshaw in *Sex and the City* – and, more recently, Maria Grazia Chiuri's "Dio(r)evolution" bag for a new millennial Dior woman, have become almost as iconic in status.

RIGHT The Dior label has moved a long way from its beginnings in society elegance – today's brand is just as much a fashionable street-style statement as a timeless go-to.

ABOVE TV shows like *Sex and the City* went a long way to popularizing the cult of the Dior handbag.

ABOVE In 1995, French President Jacques Chirac's wife, Bernadette, presented Princess Diana with an elegant black padded square Dior bag that she used so much that it was renamed the "Lady Dior" in her honour.

Fragrance
& Beauty

FINISHING TOUCHES

"Perfume is the indispensable complement to the personality of a woman, the finishing touch on a dress."
– Christian Dior

Christian Dior's love of flowers and the garden is legendary: his mother spent hours accompanied by her young son as she cultivated the garden at their first home by the sea in Granville. The houses he lived in as an adult all had wonderful gardens where he liked to sit and sketch new designs. This was especially true of his favourite home, La Colle Noir, where he grew flowers for his fragrances in the fields. Fresh flowers were abundant in the salon of his haute couture house and his designs are full of floral prints and embellishments. The scent of flowers was as seductive to the designer as their appearance, which is why perfume has been a part of the House of Dior right from its inception.

The designer founded his Christian Dior Parfums line with his childhood friend Serge Heftler-Louiche, but it was his favourite sister, Catherine, who inspired his iconic first scent. The story goes that Dior and his muse Mitzah Bricard

OPPOSITE Dior was as passionate about his fragrances as his haute couture, calling it "the finishing touch" to an outfit.

RIGHT Christian Dior's first fragrance *Miss Dior* was launched in 1947 and became an instant classic. This image from 1954 shows the Baccarat crystal bottle in which the scent was presented.

were playing with ideas for names for his debut fragrance, to be launched alongside his first haute couture collection, when his sister Catherine walked into the room. Mitzah exclaimed, "Look, there's Miss Dior!"; the English "Miss" rather than the French "Mademoiselle" spoke to the Anglophile in Dior, and he immediately proclaimed that this would be the name of his first perfume.

Miss Dior was created by Jean Carles and Paul Vacher with top notes of gardenia, galbanum, clary sage and bergamot and middle notes of carnation, iris, lily of the valley, jasmine, neroli, rose and narcissus – all the flowers that flourished in Dior's childhood beloved garden in Granville; his intention was to "create a fragrance that is like love". His sister Catherine, inspiration both in name and temperament for *Miss Dior* and to whom he was exceptionally close his whole life, was fittingly involved in the growing and providing of flowers for Dior's fragrances. The scent was an instant classic and clients of Dior began to recognize that the house perfumes were as essential to their outfit as the shoes and bags that complemented it.

Christian Dior went on to launch *Diorama* in 1949, *Eau Fraiche* in 1953 and *Diorissimo* in 1956 before his death in 1957, but under subsequent designers, many more iconic scents have been launched. These include *Diorling* (1963), *Dioressence* (1969), *Diorella* (1972), *Poison* (1985), *Dune* (1991), *Dolce Vita* (1995), *J'Adore* (1999) and *Joy de Dior* (2018) for women. In 1966, the house launched its first eau de toilette for men, *Eau Sauvage*. All the scents, whether fresh or more heavily perfumed, share a link to the beloved flowers of Dior's childhood. Dior's current "nose" is a fellow Frenchman, François Demachy. Just like Christian Dior, smell transports him immediately to his own youth – in this instance, the lavender he associates with his grandmother's

RIGHT Dior expanded its fragrance ranges into other beauty products, including talcum powder and bath oil, as early as the 1960s.

clean linens. In a 2017 interview with *The New York Times* after his creation of *J'Adore L'Or*, he explained how the creation of new perfumes still stays true to the passions of Christian Dior: "Mr Dior loved flowers like lily of the valley, so I have to keep that."

Cosmetics are also an intrinsic part of the Dior look, essential to the groomed elegance Dior sought in his designs. In 1953, then as part of Dior Parfums, a box set of eight shades of lipstick launched what would become a multimillion-euro cosmetics empire. In 1967, Serge Lutens was appointed as creative and image director of Dior cosmetics and in 1969, the first complete makeup line "L'Explosion de Couleurs" was launched. Since then, cosmetics and fragrance have become a huge revenue stream for the company, with high-profile celebrities and actresses including Marion Cotillard, Charlize Theron, Natalie Portman and Jennifer Lawrence signing lucrative deals as the face of the brand. Haute couture may be beyond the reach of most ordinary women, but fragrance and cosmetics are a way of buying a little of the Dior glamour at a fraction of the price.

RIGHT This 1972 shot shows a model with a face fully made up with the cosmetics line created in 1967 by Serge Lutens, creative and image director for Dior makeup.

BELOW Fragrance and cosmetics form a large part of Dior's revenue, promoted by multimillion-dollar advertising contracts with actresses like Natalie Portman.

INDEX

CREDITS

The publishers would like to thank the following sources for their kind permission to reproduce the pictures in this book.

Alamy: DPA Picture Alliance 73; /Everett Collection 15, 72; /Keystone Press 87b

Getty Images: AFP: 58, 95, 137; /AP 63, 67r; /Apic 12, 154l; /Archivio Cameraphoto Epoche 54; /ARNAL/PICOT/Gamma-Rapho 110, 111; /Authenticated News 92; /David Bailey/Conde Nast 155t; /Cecil Beaton/Condé Nast 84; /Serge Benhamou/Gamma-Rapho 10; /Bettmann 57, 81, 97, 102r; /Reg Birkett/Keystone 87t, 94; /Jean-Pierre Bonnotte/Gamma-Rapho 103; /BOTTI/Gamma-Rapho 102l; / Erwin Blumenfeld/Condé Nast 143; / Walter Carone/Paris Match 34; /CBS Photo Archive 17; /Chaloner Woods 153; / Chevalier 53; /Chicago History Museum 39, 56; /John Chillingworth/Picture Post/ Hulton Archive 64; /Henry Clarke/Condé Nast 49, 61; /Corbis via Getty Images 50, 100; /Jean-Claude Deutsch/Paris Match 117; /Kevork Djansezian 78r, 79; /Alfred Eisenstaedt/The LIFE Picture Collection 85; /Fox Photos 108; /Swan Gallet/WWD 133; /Jack Garofalo/Paris Match 96; /AFP/ Francois Guillot 125, 131; /Horst P. Horst/ Condé Nast 59, 144; /Housewife 152; / Hulton Archive 140; /Maurice Jarnoux/ Paris Match 66; /Gerard Julien/AFP 112; /Kammerman/Gamma-Rapho 38, 62, 150; /Keystone-France/Gamma-Keystone 22, 23, 75, 76t, 98, 101l, 101r, 109, 142; /

Claudio Lavenia 146; /Guy Marineau/ Condé Nast 118;/David McCabe/Conde Nast 104; /Frances McLaughlin-Gill 60; / Mondadori 67l; /Guy Marineau/Condé Nast 114; /Lorenzo Palizzolo 145b; / Richard Rutledge/Condé Nast 48; /Pascal Le Segretain 126, 127, 135; /Silver Screen Collection 77b; /Sunset Boulevard/Corbis 71; /Tim Graham Photo Library 89; / Laurent Van Der Stockt/Gamma-Rapho 113; /Pierre Suu 145t; /Pierre Vauthey/ Sygma 105, 107l, 116; /Victor Virgille/ Gamma-Rapho 134; /Roger Viollet 35, 37; /Kevin Winter 78l; /

Iconic Images: Norman Parkinson 36, 41, 106

Shutterstock: 119, 147r, 155b; /AP 74; / Miquel Benitez 122; /Jacques Brinon/AP 128; /Fairchild Archive/Penske Media 107r; /Granger 28, 32t, 32b, 44, 46, 52; /JALAL MorchidiI/EPA-EFE 136; /Francois Mori/ AP 121; /Tim Rooke 147r; /Roger-Viollet 7

Smithsonian Libraries: 12

V&A Images: © Cecil Beaton/Victoria and Albert Museum, London 82-83

Every effort has been made to acknowledge correctly and contact the source and/or copyright holder of each picture and the publisher apologises for any unintentional errors or omissions, which will be corrected in future editions of this book.

RESOURCES

Fury, A, Sabatini, A. (2017). *Dior Catwalk*. London: Thames & Hudson

Cullen, O., Karol Burks, C. (2019) *Christian Dior*. London: V&A Publishing

Dior, C. (1957) *Dior by Dior: The Autobiography of Christian Dior*. London: Weidenfeld & Nicolson

Cawthorne, N. (1996). *The New Look: The Dior Revolution*. London: Hamlyn

Muller, F. (2017). *Christian Dior: Designer of Dreams*. London: Thames & Hudson

dior.com

businessoffashion.com

vogue.com

thecut.com

wwd.com

en.wikipedia.org

nytimes.com

guardian.com

fashionunfiltered.com

THE LITTLE BOOK OF

CHANEL

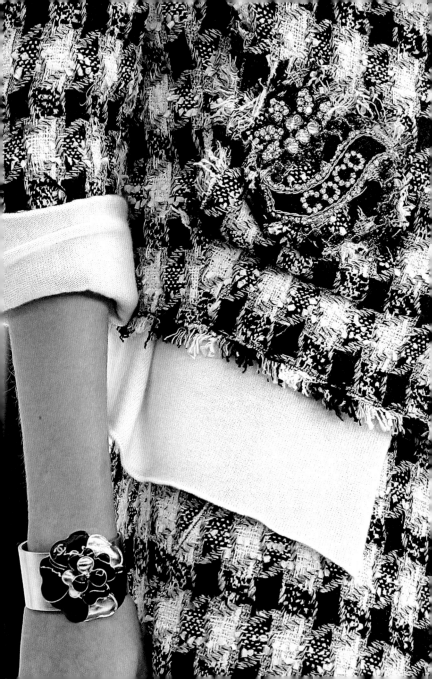

THE LITTLE BOOK OF

CHANEL

EMMA BAXTER-WRIGHT

WELBECK

Having studied fashion at St Martin's School of Art and history of art at Bristol University, Emma Baxter-Wright has taught fashion journalism at the University of the Arts London and UCA. She has contributed to many publications, including the *New York Observer, Cosmopolitan* and *Marie Claire*, and is the author of two photographic books on the English fashion photographer Brian Duffy and *Little Book of Schiaparelli*. Emma lives in London, England.

For Otis, who chose a lifestyle not an education, because it's with what cannot be taught that one succeeds.

First published in 2012 and 2017 by Carlton Books Limited
This edition published in 2020 by Welbeck
An imprint of Headline Publishing Group

Text © Emma Baxter-Wright 2012

The right of Emma Baxter-Wright to be identified as the Author of the Work has been asserted by her in accordance with the Copyright, Designs and Patents Act 1988.

A CIP catalogue record for this book is available from the British Library.

ISBN 978 1 78097 902 1

Printed in China

58

Headline's policy is to use papers that are natural, renewable and recyclable products and made from wood grown in well-managed forests and other controlled sources. The logging and manufacturing processes are expected to conform to the environmental regulations of the country of origin.

HEADLINE PUBLISHING GROUP
An Hachette UK Company
Carmelite House
50 Victoria Embankment
London EC4Y 0DZ

www.headline.co.uk
www.hachette.co.uk

Contents

Above Chanel photographed in
her suite at the Ritz Hotel in Paris,
surrounded by her famous antique
Coromandel screens, circa 1937.

Introduction

"May my legend gain ground — I wish it a long and happy life."
                                                    Coco Chanel, on her reputation

More than anyone Gabrielle "Coco" Chanel understood the value of
her own self-created mythology and she played the part brilliantly.
This exceptional and exasperating woman, who told a litany of lies to
perpetuate the ongoing mystery and confusion that surrounded her life,
was the first to recognize the couturier as a modern-day celebrity.
If the job of the couturier is to continually re-invent fashion, then Chanel
made a skilful alliance between her professional work as a designer and
her personal life story, brutally deconstructing the past, rearranging the
truth and then presenting a controlled image of herself as the role model
for what became a global brand. At a time when fashion was dominated
by male designers, she single-handedly rejected society's version of
femininity in favour of her own fabulous style, based on a functional
modern aesthetic. As one world was ending and another was about
to begin, Chanel seized the opportune moment and with visionary
insight gave women what they wanted, just before they recognized
the need. She took the basis of a man's wardrobe to create feminine
power, providing a democratic dress code that ultimately delivered
freedom, equality and understated classicism. Her status was enhanced
by her complicated personal life, which always had an impact on her
professional work, but as her rags-to-riches story unfolded, it was she
who became the influential force as a designer, lover and collaborator,
flitting seamlessly between high society and the avant-garde art set.

   A self-imposed exile of over a decade derailed her trajectory, and
that may have been the end of the fairytale, but for Chanel the vital
creativity never waned. Reinvention was part of her psyche, and when
Chanel returned to work at the age of 71 she successfully consolidated
her contribution to fashionable modernity and rebuilt her public image,
to the point that even now, many years after her death, she remains the
immovable figurehead behind the House of Chanel.

The Early Years

The details of Chanel's early life have always been shrouded in mystery and half truths, deliberately kept that way by a woman who preferred to forget, conceal and frequently provide misinformation about her miserable origins. It is often overlooked that the woman who ultimately had such a profound effect on changing the face of twentieth-century fashion, a pioneering champion of freedom and modernity, was actually born in the preceding century.

Delivered in the poorhouse on the 19 August 1883 in the small market town of Saumur, on the river Loire, Gabrielle Bonheur Chanel was the second illegitimate child of a young peasant girl called Jeanne Devolles and her wayward boyfriend Albert Chanel. Although the couple married soon after the birth, their relationship was always troubled, and when Jeanne died prematurely, Albert, who was unwilling or incapable of looking after his five children, sent the boys to work on a farm and the three girls to a convent orphanage run by nuns.

Life within the high abbey walls at Aubazine was certainly harsh for a young 12-year-old girl and, though not necessarily cruel, almost certainly without love. Gabrielle was made to wear black and it was here that she spent many hours in silent solitude, learning how to sew and potentially developing her appreciation of austere simplicity.

The girls spent their holidays with their paternal grandparents in the small garrison town of Moulins and by the age of 18 Chanel was working as a clerk in a small shop that specialized in lingerie, linen and hosiery. Early ambitions of a career on the stage were kickstarted when she began singing at various café-concerts around the town. Small, dark and distinctly different from the other girls who performed alongside

Opposite An early photograph of Chanel, aged 26, at the start of her career and before she cut her long, thick, textured hair into the trademark short bob.

her, it is thought her vaudeville repertoire consisted of only two songs: "Ko-Ko-Ri-Ko" and a vacuous ditty about a lady from Paris who had lost her puppy dog, "Qui Qu'a Vu Coco?". Her popularity grew, and soon she became known by the little word that appeared in both songs: "La petite Coco". The nickname stuck, eventually becoming synonymous with a global brand that encapsulated the ultimate in Parisienne style.

Gabrielle "Coco" Chanel was starting to gain a succession of wealthy, educated, sometimes even titled, admirers, and saw an obvious way, through her association with these men, to shake off the social stigma of poverty and enter into a higher social tier. Étienne Balsan was one such admirer; rich, attractive and without the snobbery often associated with his class, he spent his time pursuing personal pleasures and breeding racehorses. At the age of 25 Coco agreed to live with him at his estate Royallieu on the outskirts of Paris. Balsan certainly had other mistresses living with him, and Coco was known as his *irrégulière*, but through her unorthodox choice of dress she chose to differentiate herself from the other women. While most courtesans of the day still wore lavish Belle Époque-style dresses with elaborate trims and fussy frills, all of which hampered movement, Coco dressed with the utmost simplicity.

Photographs of her at this time show a young girl wearing clothes more suited to a little boy: cropped trousers, with flat boy's boots, a plain white shirt with a Peter Pan collar and a man's tie loosely knotted into a bow. With hindsight these pictures reveal a fundamental strategy, that of re-appropriating the clean uncluttered lines of classic menswear for women. Never content with a life of idle beauty, Coco kept herself busy, learning to ride and making and trimming hats for herself and her friends with some considerable success. It is hard to unravel just how happy she was, but a determination that she should never be a "kept woman" potentially fuelled the idea that she could turn her hat-making pastime into something more serious. She wanted to go to Paris and make a career for herself as a *modiste* – a milliner – and boldly suggested to Balsan that he set her up with a small shop. Although he refused her proposal, he did agree to finance a business for her from his Parisian apartment, at 160 Boulevard Malesherbes.

The dashing English millionaire Arthur "Boy" Capel was, according to Coco, the one true love of her life, and on this it is agreed she was telling the truth. Capel was a friend of Étienne Balsan's who started to appear more frequently at the chateau in the spring of 1909. He was

Opposite Exterior view of the Abbey and convent at Aubazine, where Chanel and her two sisters were placed in the orphanage and taken care of by nuns when their mother died.

Right Château de Royallieu, the grand estate outside Paris owned by Étienne Balsan, and where Chanel learnt to ride.

a charming, handsome polo-player, with an irrepressible desire for fast living and adventure. Having earned his fortune through the coalmines in northern England, he had an entrepreneurial spirit and took the idea of Coco's hat-making much more seriously than Balsan, who laughed it off as a passing fancy. For a time the trio muddled along uncomfortably, but Coco had fallen completely in love with Capel and when she ran away to live with him in Paris, the two men were left negotiating who exactly would pay what, to continue financing Coco. Finally they came to a gentlemen's agreement to share costs: Capel would cover the business expenses, while Balsan provided the premises.

Above Chanel with her lover, the Englishman Arthur "Boy" Capel, and their friend the sugar magnate Constant Say, on the beach in Saint-Jean-de-Luz in 1917.

Opposite This 1913 caricature by the satirist illustrator Sem for *Le Figaro*, shows a dancing Chanel caught in the arms of a polo-playing Boy Capel, who is depicted as a centaur.

Les Dernières Créations de la Mode

Mademoiselle Chanel was on her way. Years later she recalled to Salvador Dalí, "I was able to open a high-fashion shop because two gentlemen were outbidding each other for my hot little body." Friends and family came to buy, as did Étienne's former mistresses, all of whom were charmed by Coco's chic simple hats, which were often just bought from Galeries Lafayette and cleverly embellished. Word spread, success came almost immediately, and having outgrown the space in the apartment, Capel agreed to secure commercial premises for Coco in the centre of the established couture district. On 1 January 1910, what was to become the foundation of an empire opened its doors at 21 Rue Cambon. The sign above the door simply read "Chanel Modes".

Above Fashion illustration from the magazine *L'Élégance Parisienne,* April 1917, which shows "The Latest Fashion Creations", including hats by Chanel.

Opposite Early examples of Chanel's jersey suits. The cardigan jacket and new fuller, shorter skirt provided a suit that was far less restrictive than the extravagant fashion of her rivals.

Deauville, Biarritz, Paris

Chanel started her business selling the hats she was already making: the lease for her premises at 21 Rue Cambon stated that she had no right to make dresses as there was already a dressmaker in the same building. The hats, however, received rave reviews in the influential magazine *Les Modes* and were sought after by the popular theatre actresses and singers of the day.

Coco was a reactionary. She detested the headache-inducing hats of the fussy Belle-Époque era, heavy with plumage and gauze, so instead offered hats that relied on understated minimalism. Often they were large, but without ornate garnish; sometimes she used a single feather or grosgrain ribbon as decoration. The fashionable dress of the day was dominated by a desire for romanticism, elaborate ruffles and frilly details. The totally restrictive S-shaped corset, popular at the beginning of the century, had been challenged by the success of Paul Poiret's high-waisted empire line, but fashion was still aimed at dull society women who led inactive lives. Clothes from Jeanne Paquin, Jacques Doucet and Poiret were all heavy with colour and surface decoration, grandly sumptuous and theatrical.

Opposite Chanel loved sunbathing and swimming at the seaside. Here, she is photographed in one of her own jersey cardigans at a beach in France in 1917.

Below The familiar Chanel logo adorns the awnings of her first shop outside Paris, which opened in the fashionable seaside resort of Deauville in 1913.

Coco, who was slender and sporty, had other ideas, and her own desire to be independent provided the basis of her fledgling collection of clothes for her first boutique, which opened in Deauville in 1913. The fashionable resort on the north coast of France appealed to Coco: its component parts of dazzling sunshine, healthy sea air, wealthy men and thoroughbred horses provided her with another chance for reinvention. Financed by Boy Capel, the shop was located in the chicest part of town and had a striped awning bearing the words "Gabrielle Chanel".

Coco's first pieces were created in response to her own need to live freely and oppose women's repression. Functional clothes were inspired by the Normandy fishermen, sailor's shirts with open necks, loose linen

Right The chic coastal town of Deauville in Normandy became popular with wealthy Parisians for weekend and summer excursions during the 1920s.

Overleaf left Chanel opened her first couture house, opposite the casino in Biarritz, in July 1915, to provide a fashionable wardrobe for the cosmopolitan clientele who flocked to the Atlantic coast resort.

Overleaf right Chanel started using Rodier jersey in 1917 because it had the properties of cashmere without the expense. It draped beautifully and was perfectly suited to winter sportswear such as this stylish skater outfit from 1929.

pants, long skirts and turtleneck sweaters, all designed for comfort and ease. Encouraged by the scorching weather, Coco even made a very demure swimsuit for women to bathe in, using the soft jersey fabric she had discovered in one of Boy's sweaters. When war broke out Boy, who was called to arms, encouraged Coco to stay put and keep the shop open in Deauville. His business instincts proved to be right, as business boomed under the patronage of wealthy women who sought refuge at the seaside.

A year later, Boy swept Coco off for a weekend away in Biarritz where they stayed at the Hotel du Palais. Seemingly unaffected by war, the Basque town provided the perfect location for Coco to repeat the

success of Deauville. Here, in July 1915, she opened her first couture house in a villa facing the casino, catering for a cosmopolitan clientele who were crying out for luxury as a distraction from the brutality that surrounded them. The war had upended fashion as it existed, but Coco was inventive, improvising with available fabrics such as Rodier's knitted jersey, and producing clothes that provided a modern aesthetic as well as practicality. She understood the changing world, and while her clothes were never cheap (dresses were priced at 3,000 francs each) she had refined a new functionality that combined fluidity with pared-down elegance. Orders flowed in from Madrid, Bilbao and even the Spanish court. By the end of the war Coco was doing so well financially that she was able to reimburse Boy for his initial funding, and could finally declare her total independence. In Paris she expanded her business, moving across the road to a six-storey building at 31 Rue Cambon, which to this day remains the centre of operations for the House of Chanel.

Though inextricably linked, like the intertwining Cs of Chanel's logo, Capel and Coco had a complex love affair, bound together but pulling in different directions. Coco knew that Boy had many other liaisons and due to her social status was unlikely ever to propose, but it was a devastating blow when in 1918 he married a beautiful young aristocrat called Lady Diana Wyndham – and there was worse to come. In December 1919, Boy was fatally wounded when the speeding convertible he was driving from Paris to Monte Carlo burst a tyre and overturned. Years later Coco told her friend Paul Morand in a conversation that was published as a memoir: "In losing Capel, I lost everything. He left a void in me that the years have not filled." The reality was that a grief-stricken Coco withdrew to lick her wounds for a time. When she returned with a hardened heart, the process of renewal continued as her domination of Paris gathered pace.

Opposite This outfit is a typical example of Chanel's early modern sportswear, made in a soft jersey fabric, which ensured both comfort and freedom. The unstructured cardigan jacket became a staple piece throughout this period. Photograph by fashion and portrait photographer Dora Kallmus, known as "Madame D'Ora", in 1929.

Right Chanel designed with a limited colour palette that included black, white, beige, red and blue, as shown in this detail of a modern geometric print, circa 1929. Made from wool and silk, the fabric was used for a dress.

The House of Chanel

"Fashion is not an art, it is a job."

Coco Chanel

Coco Chanel was unlike any other designer in that she did not design on paper or make sketches. Her talent lay in her instinctive knowledge of how to dress the uncorseted female form. At the start of her career she lacked technical expertise and, having carefully chosen the fabrics, would explain verbally to her staff what she wanted. This was often a harrowing process for everyone: Coco barked orders at her assistants, and models were made to stand for hours while she endlessly pinned and repositioned the fabric until she was satisfied.

Coco understood that postwar life required simplicity and that society had changed dramatically. She was responsible for a major shift in women's fashion that relied on clean lines and mass production. Taking advantage of her social connections, she enlisted the help of the Balsan brothers to secure silk from Lyon, while Boy helped her acquire tweeds from Scotland. When fabric was difficult to source, she simply found a way to successfully utilize what was available: cotton jersey, flannel and broadcloth. Fur was impossible to find and consequently so highly in demand that clients usually didn't ask too many questions as to the origin of the skins. Coco used whatever she could get hold of, such as squirrel and white angora rabbit, for bands of fur around hemlines and cuffs.

Opposite Eveningwear in the 1930s was extravagant and luxurious. This white satin gown with a dramatic deep V back features a decorative bow, something Chanel started to incorporate on the front and back of her dresses during this period.

Left Hemlines fluctuated during the 1920s. Here, illustrated by John La Gatta for an American fashion magazine in 1925, chiffon scarves are tied round the hips and at the shoulder line to create a fashionable pointed handkerchief effect.

Everything Coco did in her personal life had an impact on the brand, as her design philosophy was based thoroughly on herself and what she liked to wear. She exemplified the *garçonne* look with her chic bobbed hair and lithe physique; she wore slim sweaters and drop-waist skirts with a pulled-down cloche hat, creating a look that became known in New York and London as "the flapper". Coco was sporty and she loved riding horses and outdoor life at the beach, which kept her slim, tanned and, by all accounts, much younger looking than her actual years. In 1920 *Vogue* magazine wrote: "Everything she does makes news – the first quilted coat, the narrow crepe de chine dress inside a cage of tulle, and the suntan which she cultivates."

During the 1920s the economy boomed for the privileged, and Chanel opened more premises to provide her wealthy clients with expensive items she had cleverly remodelled from "poor clothes". In the heart of Paris she consolidated her empire in Rue Cambon as she took over her third shop, at number 29, later adding numbers 25, 27 and 23, as well as opening another boutique in the chic Riviera town of Cannes.

Right and detail above A black silk crepe dress embellished all over with sequins and embroidery in midnight blue and light blue. The chiffon scarf attached at the back hangs slightly longer, to create the fashionable fluid hemline.

The Slav Period

Throughout her life Coco was unashamedly influenced by the men she associated with. Sergei Diaghilev, Igor Stravinsky and her new lover, the Grand Duke Dmitri Pavlovich (a handsome but penniless playboy), were all Russian émigrés who had escaped the Revolution and come to Paris, bringing with them a somewhat fictionalized version of Russian life that the French people fell in love with. Coco had complicated relationships with all three men, but was influenced by their artistic and cultural heritage, immediately sensing that romantic Russia could have great commercial appeal. Inspired, she went on to produce a collection of traditional peasant clothing that she called her "Slav period". The war had disrupted textile production and fashion houses became increasingly starved of luxury fabrics, so Coco found a way to embellish plain black crepe de chine with stunning embroidery, resulting in beautiful cloth that could rival the finest couture fabrics. The fashion world was surprised by her use of intricate embroidery but, as ever, it was the structural simplicity and wearability of these pieces that made them so popular. Sticking to a dark colour palette and then strategically embellishing with vivid colours, she made rustic-looking shift dresses, tunics and waistcoats, and reinterpreted a traditional belted blouse with a square décolletage called the "roubachka" style. The collection appeared in *Vogue* magazine in 1922 under the headline "The Peasant Look".

Opposite Taking inspiration from simple peasant shapes, Chanel created a plain black wool shift dress and used intricate gold embroidery to decorate it with simple Russian folk art, circa 1924.

Coco commissioned the sister of Dmitri, the Grand Duchess Maria Pavlovna, to produce the exquisite embroidery for her. Using the skills of the expatriate Russian community as her workforce, Maria went on to run a successful business she named Kitmir, employing about 50 women. The Kitmir atelier (who also supplied embroidery to other couturiers) initially produced everything by hand, which was both time and labour intensive. Coco demanded speed and perfection and she dismissed the idea that the folkloric embroidery had to be hand-stitched, instead providing three sewing machines for the workshop that produced comparable results more efficiently. Always a commercial innovator, Coco felt the decorative effect of the Balkan motifs lost none of their aesthetic impact simply because they were made by machine. For her the finished visual effect was more important than traditional authenticity, as was later exemplified by her extravagant use of costume jewellery.

Left The square neckline of this little black dress made from silk crepe, circa 1926–27, is typical of Chanel's "Slav period". The loose apron-like bodice, which is fastened with press-studs at the shoulders, floats over the finely pleated skirt and has long ties that fasten at the back.

Opposite This 1922 sleeveless shift dress is made from silk georgette, which flares from the hips and features the uneven hemline so popular at the time. It is decorated all over with clear glass bugle beads and metallic gold and black thread embroidery.

Flapper Dresses

The roaring, reckless Twenties went on to become known as the Jazz Age, a time when those who could afford it were hell-bent on hedonism. Cocktails, cabaret and non-stop dancing were the popular pursuits, and Chanel's tubular shift dresses, elaborately decorated with intricate beading, sequins and gold thread embroidery, were "must-have" items. Made from chiffon and tulle, these evening flapper dresses were sleeveless, fluid and flattering for the new boyish body that society women were starving themselves to achieve. Many were expertly cut in one piece to avoid ugly side seams. Hemlines were still fluctuating: there were asymmetric hems and the pointed handkerchief hem, which prettily covered all options, but Coco's instincts were to keep her dress lengths rising. Apart from the visual modernism of the slightly shorter skirt it had a functional purpose too – it was easier to dance in a dress that liberated the leg.

Opposite In the 1920s, Chanel's tubular Flapper dresses led the way. Drop-waisted with skimpy skirts, they were often heavily decorated, such as this blue silk tulle evening dress (left), which is decorated with metal sequins, and the 1925 lace dress (centre) covered in crystal beads with silk ribbon bows at the neckline and hips, 1925. The drop-waist shift dress (right), from 1925, with gathered tiers and a side sash, is made from crystal beads on silk chiffon in bright red, which was one of Chanel's favourite colours for eveningwear.

Opposite In the early 1920s, Chanel's "Slavic" period became a great success after the earlier triumph of her jersey collection. Her association with Russian, Duke Dmitri Pavlovich, inspired her to pay homage to the Russian culture. She employed Dmitri's sister, the Grand Duchess Maria, and other exiled royals to execute the fantastic hand-embroidery and decorative beadwork, which embellished her finished garments. The evening line showcased "waterfall" gowns sparkling with crystal and black jet beads, such as this black bolero and fringed paillette-embroidered dress worn by model Marion Morehouse, in the Paris apartment of Condé Nast, 1926.

Above Exquisite jet handbeading on an ivory Chanel column dress from 1919. Art Deco played a prominent role in the fashion trends of the 1920s with geometric shapes based along natural lines.

Previous pages By the mid-1930s there was a definite return of the waist to its normal position, and eveningwear, which tended to be body moulding, was longer again. Taffeta, velvet, silk and lace were the preferred fabrics and Chanel often complemented her romantic evening dresses with ribbon and flower decorations and also white carnation headdresses, as seen here on the right.

Left This crepe-de-chine evening gown from the early 1930s is printed with a stark floral design of white leaves and foliage against a dark background. Pleated panels, cut on the bias to allow fluid movement, are incorporated into the front and back of the skirt, and the flounced sleeves are cut from petal-shaped panels.

Opposite Chanel made it her signature to use the same fabric for a dress or a blouse that she used to line the jacket or coat. This green muslin coat with its loose, unstructured opening is lined with silk, using the same "falling leaf" print for the matching dress, circa 1927.

Opposite For this black silk tulle evening dress from the early 1930s, Chanel has used intricate beading work and swags of gold sequins to decorate it. It is gently flared from below the hips in four tiers to allow ease of movement.

Right A fashion illustration featured in *Vogue* magazine shows Madame Paul Dubonnet wearing a black sequinned evening gown by Chanel, circa 1934.

Opposite and detail above Unlike
other industrial processes, which
Chanel felt could not compete
with hand-crafted skills, machine
lace kept its key characteristics
of elegance, lightness and luxury,
and was cheaper to produce. This
figure-hugging lace evening dress
with three-quarter length sleeves

split from the inner elbow and
gently gored skirt, is made from
intricate panels cut into the body
of the dress and dates from 1935.
The skinny waist belt (above)
was designed as part of the dress.
The metallic snap fastening is
covered with white lead glass and
translucent blue glass beads.

The English Influence

By the mid-1920s Art Deco dominated interior design and architecture, and the tubular lines of this movement were mirrored in the narrow silhouette of women's fashion. Coco had always hated ostentatious theatricality and as the decade progressed she honed her style, simplified her designs and used less and less surface decoration in her work. Her ten-year love affair with the Duke of Westminster (known at the time as the richest man in England) resulted in collections that were heavily influenced by sporting fixtures of the English aristocracy. During her time with him, Coco went fishing, shooting and sailing, and was often photographed wearing an assortment of his tweed hunting jackets, shirts and waistcoats. The cardigan, which became a wardrobe staple for fashionable women everywhere, is said to have derived from the English cricket field. In Coco's hands it became an item that was multifunctional; made from fine-knit jersey, it was easy to wear over a slim straight skirt but also purposefully useful as she ensured the pockets were actually big enough to use. Fishing trips to Scotland with the Duke introduced Coco to traditional Fair Isle patterns and Scottish tweeds, both of which were quickly appropriated into her upcoming collections.

Opposite Chanel with her lover, Hugh Richard Arthur Grosvenor, the Duke of Westminster, at the Grand National racetrack in Liverpool, March 1925. Chanel wears a cloche hat and heavy hand-knitted beige stockings.

Right The Prime Minister of Britain, Winston Churchill (right), with his son Randolph and Chanel at a boar hunt, the Mimizan Hunt, in northern France, 1928.

CHANEL

Buttoned bodices, with basques cut full, or flat, are Chanel's contribution to the winter fashion picture. Watch her little collars, fitted close to the throat and frequently faced, or doubled with another colour.

The black woollen dress on the left with white collar and cuffs, is fastened with clips at the shoulders and wrists. A red leather collar and belt of the same, bring novelty to the light navy check-woven woollen dress, while an interlaced leather belt adorns the raspberry wool marocain frock.

The first example of a Chanel suit that could be called an early template for the classic item we recognize today came in the mid-1920s, proof if it were needed that real style is timeless. Early incarnations of the suit were made of a soft wool jersey called kasha and textured tweeds. Coco usually included a three-piece ensemble for each new season, which consisted of a skirt that contained a slight flare to facilitate movement, a jacket, sometimes trimmed with matching fur collar and cuffs, and a silk satin blouse. Her attention to detail was meticulous: the jacket would be lined using the same fabric as the blouse, hours were spent perfecting the fit of the sleeve, which provided total ease of movement, and the inside was stitched as beautifully as the outside. From these formative versions the Chanel suit went on to become an instantly recognizable standard of understated elegance.

Previous left Here, in 1936, Chanel looks comfortably stylish in one of her early suits, casually belted at the waist and with workable pockets. She rarely appeared without her trademark accessory of several ropes of pearls.

Previous right This 1937 print advertisement for Chanel of three outfits shows meticulous grooming and attention to detail in collars, cuffs and belts. The silhouette is fitted, with broad shoulders and a definite return to the waist. Skirts are slimline with just a small flair for movement; these afternoon day dress show the hem dropped almost to the ankle.

Opposite A 1930s woman's magazine advertisement for Chanel showing outfits from her new spring/summer collection. The fitted coat-frock in white cotton pique and the pink organdie suit, which has all-over white embroidery, are both decorated with oversized bows at the neck, a favourite Chanel detail at the time. The slim-fitting silk jersey dress in black-and-white "*pieds-de-poule*" (a fake weave) uses crisp white cotton piqué for the reveres, hat and gloves.

WITH THAT FRESH-FROM-THE-WASH LOOK!

CHANEL

Chanel has gambled on the weather. She has thrown us all into muslins and piqués. In this suit in pink organdie embroidered in white, with a little pink blouse and pink organdie hat, you see how simple and fresh a girl may look on a midsummer day. Rather amusing for a wedding!

On the left you see one of her models in white piqué, fresh as the morning, with a hat to match. The coat-frock in all kinds of woollen materials we have had, but not in white piqué until Chanel set the fashion.

For something less in need of washing there is this silk jersey dress in black and white *pieds de poule*, or what we would call a sort of dim check. White piqué gloves, hat and revers give the freshness which Chanel exacts this summer.

The Little Black Dress

Chanel will also be forever associated with "the little black dress", although if there was a clear moment of inspiration behind the iconic fashion item, it was never revealed. Certainly there was outspoken contempt for the garish ostentatious designs of other couturiers. In her memoirs, as recounted by Paul Morand, Coco declared, "All those gaudy, resuscitated colours shocked me; those reds, those greens, those electric blues, the entire Rimsky-Korsakov palette brought back into fashion by Paul Poiret made me feel ill." She went on to elaborate that while the vivid costumes of the Ballets Russes were perfect for the stage, they were not for couture. Perhaps it came about through a moment of nostalgia related to her childhood in the orphanage at Aubazine, where she spent so much time alone in her miserable dark uniform? Or a reminder of the hellish abyss she fell into after the death of her great love. Boy Capel? Whatever the source, Chanel launched a range of little black dresses in 1926, and like so many of her classic statement pieces it was an item she returned to time and time again to adapt and tweak, endlessly reinventing the ultimate in deceptive simplicity. Chanel was not the only designer to use black, but she was the first to use the colour in such a discreet way, for both day- and eveningwear. Her early dresses were made from wool, or marocain for the day, and dull silk crepe, as well as satin crepe, of which she used both the dull and shiny side, for the evening. The cut was strikingly simple and modern, a sheath dress that hugged the contours of the body without gimmicks or excess of any sort. American *Vogue* in October 1926 dubbed the new black crepe de chine dress "the Ford dress", alluding to the mass-produced Ford motor car and predicting, correctly, that it would become standard uniform for the masses.

Opposite In the late 1920s, fashion followed the sleek, modern lines of the Art Deco movement, and Chanel invented the first of many little black dresses. This illustration from *Vogue* in April 1927 depicts Mme J M Sert in a georgette creation, with her magnificent triple-length chain of diamonds. The overcoat the gazelle hound wears is also by Chanel.

Above From the 1930s, the narrow tubular line of the *garçonne* dress started to flare slightly to allow greater freedom of movement for dancing, as can be seen in this advertisement for the House of Chanel in Paris during this period.

Opposite Published in the American edition of *Vogue* in 1926, this illustration typifies the Chanel look. The model wears a long-sleeved black dress, with detailed tucks that cross in the front, pearl earrings and necklace, and a tall black cloche hat. This angular, unembellished style of dressing caused Paul Poiret to comment that Chanel had invented "Poverty de luxe".

"Look for the woman in the dress. If there is no woman, there is no dress."

Coco Chanel

Costume Design

Misia Sert was an extraordinary woman who was capable of bringing out the creative genius in people. She was the only real friend Coco ever had, although their longstanding friendship was not without the occasional explosive outburst. Married to the Catalan artist José-Maria Sert and connected to an impressive circle of writers, musicians and artists, to whom she was both a muse and confidante, Misia acted as a creative conduit within the Parisian art scene. As a couple, the Serts were both instrumental in developing Coco's understanding and appreciation of art, and through their friendship Coco came into contact with Sergei Diaghilev, Léon Bakst, Jean Cocteau, Pablo Picasso, Erik Satie and Ivor Stravinsky, among others.

The prolific and multitalented Jean Cocteau (writer, poet, designer, painter and film-maker) was the first to recognize Chanel's potential as a costume designer, and in 1923 asked her to design for his production of the classical Greek tragedy *Antigone*. It was Coco's first foray into theatre and her geometric prints, based on Greek motifs, and subtle colour palette, highlighted with brick red, cleverly complemented the backdrops, which were designed by Picasso. The play completely baffled audiences but Chanel's costumes received good reviews from the critics.

Her next, and perhaps most famous, theatrical contribution came in 1924 when Diaghilev asked her to collaborate with Cocteau on his idea for the Ballets Russes' *Le Train Bleu*. Diaghilev's groundbreaking production combined ballet with acrobatics, satire and pantomime, resulting in a show described as "danced operetta". A new era of modernism prevailed; the Cubist sculptor Henri Laurens produced the stage sets and Picasso illustrated the programme. Rejecting the idea

Opposite The Hollywood actress Ina Claire (left), pictured here with Chanel in 1931, looked stunning in a Chanel outfit in the 1930 movie *The Royal Family of Broadway*.

Within the image, the following text is visible on posters:

MACB[
Tragédie de William S
Traduite et adaptée par Front
Décors et costumes de Je
Musique de scène de Guy D
Mise en scène de Julie

ŒDI

de SOPHOC
adopté par Jean CC
Mise en scène et costumes de
Costumes féminins de Mme C
Décors de Guillaum
Régisseur du groupe : Phi

LA MACHINE
INFERNALE

JEAN COCTEAU

Opposite Chanel is pictured here with her best friend Misia Sert (centre), on the Lido beach in Venice in 1929. Misia acted as a creative conduit for Chanel, introducing her to a wide circle of artistic and aristocratic people.

Above Jean Cocteau, seen here in his hotel bedroom in 1937 sketching the model Elizabeth Gibbons in a sequinned Chanel dress, was introduced to Chanel through their mutual friend Misia Sert. They collaborated on many artistic projects, and Cocteau called her "the greatest couturière of our time".

of stage costume, Coco chose instead to put the dancers in real sports clothes from her current collection – swimsuits, drop-waist shift dresses and striped sweaters. She did not adapt the loose-fitting knits (always a Chanel staple) for stage performance and, unsurprisingly, the dancers found it hard to firmly grasp and hold each other during the complex routines. The couturier gave no concession to the artistic requirements of the performers – and even expected them to dance wearing rubber bathing slippers! However, Chanel went on to design costumes for a series of ballet performances called *Les Soirées de Paris* at the Théâtre de la Cigale produced by her old friend Étienne de Beaumont, and would later again collaborate with both the Ballets Russes and Cocteau.

Opposite Ballet dancers Lydia Sokolova and Leon Woizikwsky in the 1924 Diaghilev production for the Ballets Russes of *Le Train Bleu*. Jean Cocteau conceived the story and Chanel designed the knitted costumes, which caused great problems for the dancers who found it difficult to grasp each other.

Right Chanel collaborated with the Spanish artist Salvador Dalí on the ballet he designed with Diaghilev's Ballet Russes de Monte Carlo. Set to the music of Wagner's "Tannhauser", Chanel is seen here putting the final touches to the costume of Mad King Ludwig of Bavaria, who is the central character in *Bacchanale*, which was premiered at the Metropolitan Opera House in New York in 1940.

The Hollywood Connection

In the meantime, complicated negotiations with Hollywood were underway. To be connected in some way with the ultra-chic style of Mademoiselle Chanel gave a production an added dimension of glamour, and it was this that the movie magnate Samuel Goldwyn was determined to tap into when, through the Russian Dmitri, he stage-managed a meeting with Coco in Monte Carlo. Goldwyn wanted Chanel to provide some understated Parisian glamour for his leading ladies, but he also wanted her to refine American's tastes in fashion, and planned that all his stars should not only be dressed by Chanel in his movies but also in their private lives. At a time when America was suffering financially, he was furious that his female stars were flaunting conspicuous extravagance, and thought with Chanel on board he could win back public approval. In the 1930 movie *The Royal Family of Broadway*, Ina Claire had already appeared wearing a stunning black Chanel suit with a red fox fur trim, but Goldwyn's new deal for Coco asked for a much bigger commitment on both sides. After many months of protracted negotiations he offered her a guaranteed contract of $1 million dollars, which seemed too good to turn down, and Coco finally set off for Hollywood with Misia in 1931. There she was greeted with much acclaim and introduced to Hollywood royalty: Greta Garbo, Marlene Dietrich, Claudette Colbert and the directors George Cukor and Erich von Stroheim. Her visit was short, and somewhat volatile, as she let it be known that she would not be told what to do by the studio system and that she would be designing everything in Paris, sending a team of assistants to the studios in California to complete fittings. Having worked so hard to gain total independence in her business, Coco found it impossible to put herself up for hire and be subordinate

Right Chanel's association with Hollywood was shortlived, but she was responsible for designing the costumes for Gloria Swanson in *Tonight or Never* in 1931 which also starred Melvyn Douglas.

to the female stars of Hollywood, who in turn refused to have her style imposed upon them.

In the end she worked on just three films – *Palmy Days* (1931), *The Greeks Had a Word for Them* (1932), and *Tonight or Never* (1931) starring Gloria Swanson. None were huge box-office hits, although Chanel's creations for Swanson were praised in the press. *The New Yorker* noted her return to Europe by saying her dresses were simply not sensational enough: "She made a lady look like a lady. Hollywood wants a lady to look like two ladies."

Above A still from the movie *The Greeks Had a Word for Them*, which starred Joan Blondell and Ina Claire, both wearing costumes designed by Chanel. This was the last film Chanel worked on, as she found the Hollywood experience restrictive and uncreative.

Opposite *Palmy Days* was the first movie for which Chanel was contracted to design costumes. Starring Charlotte Greenwood and Eddie Cantor, the musical comedy was not a huge hit, and Chanel was required to deliver little more than a few dresses for the leading lady.

War & Exile

During the 1930s, the House of Chanel continued to seduce Paris and the wider world, but the decade was not without hiccups. In 1936 Chanel's workforce went on strike to demand more money. Unwilling to negotiate, a furious Coco, who felt betrayed by their disloyalty, fired the whole team. The women who refused to leave had a "sit in" at the Rue Cambon premises until Coco finally capitulated, but the story sparked unwelcome publicity. There was also real competition from the exuberant Italian couturier Elsa Schiaparelli, who was based in Paris. Her witty creations, infused with shocking colour and surreal gimmicks, were diametrically opposed to everything Chanel represented, but while Coco dismissed her as "that Italian woman who makes dresses", the fashion press adored her, and she undoubtedly eclipsed some of Chanel's glory.

Despite ongoing disappointments and tragedy in her personal life, Coco, at 56, showed no signs of retiring, so it seemed a surprisingly knee-jerk reaction to the declaration of war in 1939 to immediately choose to close down the House of Chanel. The government wanted all the couture houses to stay open for French propaganda purposes, and many did, but Coco was unequivocal. She laid off all her employees without notice and decided only the boutique that sold perfume would remain open. She immediately fled the city and took refuge in the south of France for several months, before returning to Paris in the middle of 1940.

Although Coco arrived to find the swastika flying over the entrance to the Ritz Hotel, and all the rooms requisitioned by German military, her connections secured her a room and she still had her

Opposite Chanel, standing next to her dressing table in her apartment in the Ritz Hotel, Paris, in 1937, with fashion illustrations pinned to the wall.

Left Chanel used colour sparingly and usually offset it with black, as here in this dress of high contrasts that has a bodice and centre panel of bright metallized lace in green and candy pink, highlighted over a narrow skirt of dull black crepe.

Opposite A 1938 Jean Cocteau illustration of a stunning Chanel evening gown, made from black Valenciennes lace with decorative flower patterns and trimming made from iridescent paillettes.

private apartment at 31 Rue Cambon. Wartime shortages enforced improvisation, at which Coco was already an expert; she lived discreetly but scandalized Paris by having an affair with a good-looking German who was very much younger than her. Hans Günther von Dincklage (known as "Spatz") was tall, handsome and accustomed to the good life. His exact role in the war remains ambiguous; he was known to work as an attaché to the German embassy in Paris, but persistent rumours suggest he was a spy, working as a double agent for both the Nazis and the British. Despite loud protestations that she did not collaborate with the Germans (Coco always claimed Spatz was

Iridescent paillettes on a black
Valenciennes lace dress. Chanel.

English, as they spoke the language to each other and his mother was English), he was not the only German that she had dealings with. British Intelligence papers that are now declassified show that Coco was involved in an extraordinary covert mission called "Operation Modellhut" (fashion hat), which she undertook in strictest secrecy early in 1944. Boasting of her great friendship with Winston Churchill (an acquaintance from the many years she'd spent with the Duke of Westminster), Coco suggested she could act as an intermediary, and use her persuasive powers to encourage Churchill to enter peace talks with the German government. The implausible plan was given the go-ahead, and Coco travelled to Madrid to meet the English ambassador who was to be an integral part of the plot. Whatever her real intentions, Coco's assessment of her relationship with Churchill seems fantastically overstated, and the mission fizzled out.

Two weeks after the Liberation of France, Coco was arrested in her room at the Ritz by the Forces Françaises de l'Intérieur. Punishment for collaboration was brutal, suspects were imprisoned for months, women had their heads shaved and were paraded in the streets; many others were simply shot. Coco was more fortunate. It is thought that intervention from the Duke of Westminster via Winston Churchill saved her, and she was released after just a few hours. The French people were less willing to forgive her romantic liaisons with the enemy and her reputation, which for so long had been untouchable, was now severely damaged. In 1945 Coco left for Switzerland, where Spatz soon joined her. She stayed there for eight long years, an exile who visited the United States occasionally and returned to Paris only for brief visits.

Opposite left Featured in the 1938–9 collection, this was one of the last Chanel dresses created before the outbreak of war. The edge of the silk chiffon and grosgrain bodice is trimmed with red, white and blue grosgrain ribbon, the colour of the Tricolour, worn over a matching red silk chiffon skirt.

Above A revealing black taffeta
evening gown has a fitted corselet
bodice strapped with long ribbons
that wrap around the body and
tie in huge bows at the hips. The
bouffant skirt is made from panels
of black silk net, but attention
focuses on the cutaway straps and
a daringly low neckline.

1937 - Robe du soir

The Incomparable Coco, Mademoiselle Chanel,
her white crepe dinner dress her magnificent
multicolored jewels and her hair ribbon.

Jean Cocteau
☆ 1937

Opposite In Rome with Jean Cocteau and their friend Miss Weiseveiller. Cocteau became one of Chanel's most trusted friends.

Above Illustration by Jean Cocteau of Chanel, 1937, wearing a white crepe dinner dress, accessorized with her trademark enamel cuffs.

Left Cocteau produced endless beautiful line drawings of Chanel's dress designs, many of which were commissioned for publication in the prestigious fashion journals of the day. This backless evening gown, designed by Cocteau for Chanel, circa 1939, has an elaborate frill print.

CHANEL

A DRESS BY CHANEL, OF AN EXTRAORDINARY PRINT I
SIGNED BY JEAN COCTEAU, IN ROSE, BLACK AND WHIT

Chanel

White marocain twinkling with
black paillettes, a black ribbon
belt and a mad coiffure con-
cocted of ribbon, feathers and
a pailletted veil.

Jean ✷

Robe de Chanel. Ruban
marocain blanc. fleurs de
paillettes noires.

Coiffure de rubans
plumes en paillettes.
voilette pailletée.

Paris

1937

Above In another illustration by
Cocteau, this Chanel design from
1937 is made in white marocain
and decorated with twinkling
black paillettes. The extravagant
hairpiece, made of ribbon, feathers
and a pailletted veil, is not typical
of Chanel's understated style.

The Triumphant Return

The House of Chanel had been closed for 14 years, and the exceptional success of its founder had long since passed into fashion history, when Coco, who was now over 70, made the momentous decision to relaunch her career. There were many reasons behind her decision: it is thought her time in exile had left her lonely and bored and she desperately missed the work she loved, which she always claimed "consumed her life". Sales of her perfume *Chanel No. 5* were in decline and needed a publicity boost, and perhaps more pertinently she was horrified at the postwar success of Christian Dior's "New Look". Coco was outspoken in her views, having worked so hard to release women from the tyranny of theatrical dress, and it infuriated her now to see Dior being worshipped for his restrictive silhouette that once again subordinated women's bodies to a male view of femininity. She felt the time was right to reinstate her original ethos: to provide clothes that simplified choice, offered women comfort and understated elegance and which liberated the female body.

In 1953, in preparation for her new collection, Coco went back to 31 Rue Cambon, where she refurbished the boutique that sold her perfume as well as reinstated the workrooms and her famous third-floor apartment. She presented her new collection of 130 models on 5 February 1954 (the date was significant because five was always her lucky number).

The fashion press anticipated fantastic things from the House of Chanel – and then damningly delivered their verdict. Almost unanimously the European papers derided her collection as dull and disappointing, the reviews savage in their condemnation: "a Fiasco"…

Opposite That instantly recognizable classic, the Chanel suit, is photographed outside the boutique in Rue Cambon in 1959. The trademark accessories of pearls, white gloves, flat hat and slingback shoes complete the look.

"a melancholy retrospective"… "a flop". Lesser women would have been crushed by the criticism, but not Coco, who was back at her workroom within a few days with a renewed determination to go on and prove her point. Europe may have dismissed her, but the American press showed enthusiastic support by running features on the new collection in the March issues of both American *Vogue* and *Life* magazines. The American public liked what they saw, and orders from the states flooded in. Women were responding to what Chanel offered them: less-conspicuous "fashion" and instead a rather more modern attitude to functional style. As each new collection appeared, the essence of the Chanel phenomenon gathered speed. She remained faithful to the neutral colour palette she loved – beige, black, white, red and navy – and used the same classic fabrics: tweeds, jersey, satin brocades, velvet and lamé for evening. Her 1950s suits were significantly more tailored than her earlier cardigan suits, and she was now incorporating the styling details that would ultimately come to define the "Chanel look".

By 1958, with Dior dead, British *Vogue* proclaimed: "Chanel is the major fashion influence in the world. Her jersey suits and blazer jackets are copied all down the line to the local high street, and she is responsible for the popularity of men's shirts, jewelled cufflinks and medallions, gilt and pearl earrings, Breton sailor hats, and slingback shoes with contrasting toe-caps."

Opposite A Chanel suit from the year Coco made her comeback in 1954. The outfit in navy blue jersey, with its plain white shirt, man's bowtie and Breton-style sailor hat, embodies much of the androgyny that Chanel championed for women.

Overleaf left White organza and silver strapless dress with a layered skirt dates from the mid-1950s. Silver leaves edge the neckline of the bodice and the tiers of the skirt.

Overleaf right Cocktail dresses, like this one in black lace, featured regularly in Chanel's collections in the late 1950s and early 1960s. The strapless, boned dress, from 1958, has a trumpet-shaped skirt with a triple flounce.

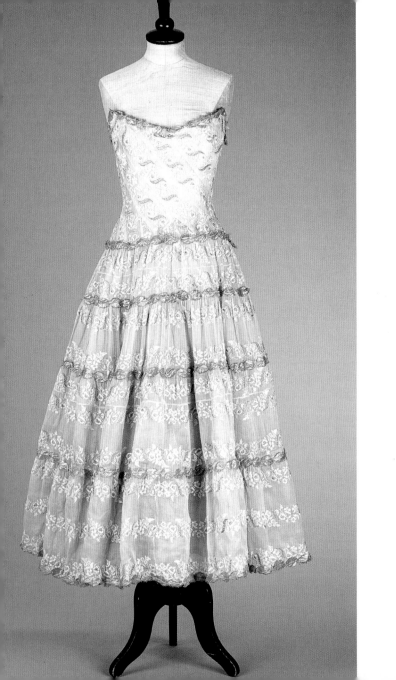

The Chanel Suit

The head-to-toe look, which was instantly recognizable, flew in the face of "fashion" and remains utterly timeless, began with the Chanel suit. Whatever the detailed variations, proportions are visually balanced. The soft boxy jacket was easy to wear, unstructured and yet had so many trademarks. It was always identifiable by the gold chain stitched to the hem of the lining that guaranteed a perfect hang, the overstitching of the lining that ensured the inside of the jacket was just as elegant as the outside, and the buttonholes, which were never fake. In keeping with her personal taste, all the embossed buttons were made to be functional as well as decorative, often designed to look like jewellery. Gilt buttons were particular favourites; they could be traced with the double-C logo or a lion's head, which originated from Coco's astrological star sign Leo.

Opposite Fashion illustrations for the iconic Chanel tweed jacket by Karl Lagerfeld.

Above A 1964 Chanel mauve tweed jacket with double pockets has a silk floral lining, turned over to trim the collar, patch pockets and front opening.

Left Chanel dismissed the Youthquake antics of 1960s fashion, and carried on honing her style. This signature suit from autumn/ winter 1965 has a collarless boxy jacket, with three-quarter-length sleeves and numerous pockets; the skirt length has crept up to above the knee.

Some jackets were collarless, others had neat narrow lapels or stand-up Nehru collars – and the fit of the sleeve was paramount. Coco maintained the sleeve was the most important part of the garment, and would spend hours repositioning the shoulder and sleeve seams to achieve perfection. Her suit jackets always included real pockets because they were needed to hold Mademoiselle's cigarettes. Coco added braid to the jackets of her suits and very often utilized the same fabric for other details, edging a pocket, adding a fake cuff, trimming a button or lining the suit.

This winning formula of a short, square, collarless jacket worn with a slightly flared skirt that cut across the knee became the signature piece for the House of Chanel, and while no two suits were exactly the same, she repeated this particular concept endlessly, subtly reworking through the same style themes to provide her customers with a classicism that went beyond that season's fashion. Added to this were the trademark finishing touches that continually reinforced Coco's personal signature: layers of jewels, glass stones or pearls, sometimes just a few neat strings around the neck, occasionally more flamboyant; the gently rounded two-tone slingback shoes with a delicate heel and black cap toe, designed to visually shorten the foot, and the perfectly placed hat, usually small with a simple ribbon tied into a bow at the back or a camellia perched on the side. These are the essential elements that together add up to the success of the look.

Opposite top The soft tweed couture suit (left) is lined in quilted cream cotton jersey and worn with a cream wool sleeveless bodice underneath the collarless jacket, which has double pockets on both sides, decorated with Chanel buttons. The salmon pink dress and jacket (right) is lined in pink chine taffeta, which is also used for the piping detail on the pockets and cuff. Both circa 1960s.

Opposite Chanel was one of the first couturieres to put women in trousers. Here, in a mid-1960s ensemble, she successfully mixes textures, using soft white wool for the sleeveless vest and trousers, with an oversized diaphanous shirt.

Right The masculine lines of this 1960s black trouser suit are softened by the ice blue silk used to line the jacket and create the blouse. Chanel often designed fake cuffs for sleeves, using the same fabrics she had used for other details; here, the blue silk is used as a tie to belt the trousers, wrapping into a decorative bow.

Overleaf left By the mid-1960s a Chanel jacket was coveted by fashionable women the world over who wanted to buy into her "casual chic", like this pink and blue tartan jacket with fringed collar and fringed sleeve seams, photographed for *Queen* magazine.

Overleaf right A salmon pink and cream woollen dress, cut to the knee, is worn with the matching collarless jacket. Complementary shades are used to trim the jacket edges, sleeve opening and for the chevron-shaped pockets. Gilt buttons fasten the opening.

Celebrity Connections

The postwar suit became the stylish uniform for elegant women of a certain age who needed Parisian panache. Jackie Kennedy was already a customer of Chanel (as well as many other French couture houses) before her husband became President of the United States, having ordered from Chanel from 1955 onwards. On the fatal trip to Dallas with JFK in November 1963, she was wearing a favourite Chanel suit that she had worn before. Made to order from the autumn/winter 1961 couture collection, the vivid pink suit made from textured wool had a short double-breasted jacket with three-quarter-length sleeves, double pockets on the front, edged with navy taffeta and gold buttons. Jackie was sitting alongside her husband in the open-top limousine when three bullet shots rang out and the president was killed. The First Lady, covered in blood and gore, stayed in her Chanel suit all day, and the pictures broadcast around the world remain the enduring image of a tragic day.

Chanel was now the label that everyone wanted to be seen in, and it was not just the chic European stars that flocked to Rue Cambon. Great French beauties like Jeanne Moreau, Brigitte Bardot and Anouk Aimée all endorsed her signature style; the film director Luchino Visconti (whom Coco knew from a brief affair in the 1930s) introduced her to a young ingénue called Romy Schneider, who she dressed for Visconti's section of the 1962 film *Boccaccio '70*. On the other side of the Atlantic, the big names in Hollywood were just as keen to flaunt the label, as a Chanel outfit implied chic glamour without screaming "showbiz". Elizabeth Taylor never looked so good as when she appeared in a tailored Chanel suit. Lauren Bacall, Grace Kelly, Ingrid Bergman, Marlene Dietrich – these were women who were regularly named as the best-dressed women in the world, and their choice of designer was Chanel.

Opposite Jackie Kennedy in a pink wool Chanel suit and hat, with her husband President John F Kennedy, arriving at Dallas airport on that tragic day in November 1963.

Previous page left White was used to great effect for short cocktail dresses and eveningwear throughout the 1960s: Chanel herself said, "Dress women in black or white at a ball. They will catch the eye". Here the boned bodice fits the body like a glove, and then flares out dramatically from the hips with a full skirt with horizontal layers of ruffles, designed to emphasize the shape.

Previous page right Silver and white were colours that dominated the early 1960s. Chanel captured the mood for evening by using contrasting textures of shiny sequins, iridescent pearls and frothy layers of white tulle.

Right For much of her life Chanel lived in a three-roomed apartment above the shop at 31 Rue Cambon, surrounded by her precious books, the lacquered Coromandel screens and the crystal chandelier she designed herself. A Greek marble dating from the fifth century BC on the mantelpiece and two Chinese bronze deer, dating from the eighteenth century, both are indications of the designer's wealth. She is pictured here in 1965.

Previous page left Through the years, the signature style remained elegant and inevitably incorporated the essential details that Chanel had made her trademark. The cream floral-print fabric from the shift dress re-appears in the lapels and coat lining, while the flat hat is made from the same dusky pink wool as the coat.

Previous page right Variations on a white theme from the mid-1960s. Layers of crisp organza are offset with a silk taffeta sash and bow in contrasting colours and silver cap-toe shoes.

Left New proportions for the suit in 1963: a slim skirt cut to below the knee with straight seven-eighths coat made in bright wool. Luxurious grey mink trims the collar and cuffs, and two rows of small gilt buttons are used for the double-breasted opening.

Opposite Brown cape and dress ensemble, with a matching hat, from the 1960s. Mink lines the cape and trims the collar and brim of the hat. The model wears pearl stud earrings and one of Chanel's innovative pieces of costume jewellery the pendant cross, set with pearls and heavy glass stones.

Above Illustrations of two of Chanel's dress designs from around 1965 both show a shorter silhouette in response to the changing times.

Opposite A vibrant turquoise and pink, silk, print dress, worn with an off-white wool jacket, uses matching fabric for pocket, cuffs and lining. The Breton-style hat is reminiscent of the very first styles Chanel wore as a young girl.

Overleaf left Coco Chanel, celebrating backstage after a show surrounded by models, all of whom were chosen because they resembled Mademoiselle and exemplified the house style.

Overleaf right In the workroom Chanel was rarely seen without a pair of long scissors hanging on a ribbon around her neck. Models were expected to stand for hours while she scrutinized the fit and eliminated any flaws.

The End of an Era

Coco kept working up until the very end. The Swinging Sixties seemed an irrelevance to someone who had carved out such a distinguished career based on elegant modernity as opposed to fashionable trends; she simply ignored the obsession with youth and carried on in her own indomitable way. In the final years, Coco had a small retinue of staff to look after her in her rooms at the Ritz Hotel; she was extraordinarily wealthy, but having sacrificed her personal life to work, and with so many of her friends gone, she became increasingly isolated and lonely. Coco Chanel died in her room at the Ritz on Sunday, 10 January 1971. She was 88 years old. The funeral service, which was attended by all the great and the good of the fashion world including Yves Saint Laurent, Pierre Balmain and Cristóbal Balenciaga, as well as Salvador Dalí and Jeanne Moreau, took place at L'Eglise de la Madeleine, the grandest church next to Rue Cambon. As her final resting place she requested the cemetery in Lausanne, Switzerland.

Opposite This long white evening dress from 1970 was the last dress Chanel ever made for herself. Understated in its simplicity, it was made from white silk chiffon, worn over a fine white silk knit strapless petticoat. She wore it on several occasions before she died.

Overleaf Models from the House of Chanel were among mourners who attended the memorial service at L'Eglise de la Madeleine. Chanel died in her bedroom at the Ritz Hotel, 10 January 1971.

The Lagerfeld Years

"Coco always borrowed from the boys. She took their jackets, and made them into uniforms for women." Karl Lagerfeld

With the death of Coco, the House of Chanel stagnated for a while. Without the commander-in-chief, the empire lurched onwards, lacking direction but still supported by a continually ageing clientele who remained faithful to Chanel's classic style. It was not until 12 years later, with the arrival of Karl Lagerfeld in 1983, that the House of Chanel once again emerged as a creative and extraordinarily influential force. The prolific German fashion designer, who also worked for Chloé, Krizia and Max Mara, and produced collections for Fendi, his own label Karl Lagerfeld, and both haute couture and ready-to-wear for Chanel, was an inspirational choice to continue the legacy that Coco worked so hard to establish.

Affectionately known in the fashion press as "King Karl", Lagerfeld breathed new life into the memory of Coco Chanel for nearly 30 years. Under his masterful leadership Chanel rose phoenix-like to a position of worldwide dominance. His genius lay in incorporating a younger funkier edge into the collections, to broadening the mass appeal of the brand, while simultaneously retaining the established slightly older market who expected the label to be synonymous with impeccable quality, elegance and understatement.

Opposite Karl Lagerfeld seen here at work, sketching designs, in his studio in Paris, April 1983.

Left Lagerfeld incorporated all the iconic Chanel symbols into his work, taking inspiration from the motifs he found on the famous Coromandel screens and reworking them with exquisite embroidery for autumn/winter 1993–4.

Opposite Karl Lagerfeld with the model Stella Tennant, dressed in a lavishly embroidered black evening coat depicting the intricate images of birds of paradise, waterfalls, temples and cherry blossom, all found on the Chinese Coromandel screens that Chanel kept in her apartment. From the haute couture autumn/winter 1996–7 collection.

Lagerfeld's mission statement was to work around the elements of Chanel's original concepts, using what he found in the archives as a springboard to reinterpreting and rejuvenating what had, in truth, become safe and predictable. Initially he made scrapbooks that contained every visual reference to anything that was connected to Chanel's history (see page 113). He used these as a point of reference, acknowledging the spirit of the past, and then absorbed and rejected as necessary, with the ultimate intention of producing something disconcertingly new. Lagerfeld didn't do nostalgia. Rather, he had the ability to skilfully juggle the connective threads between the past, present and future. While acknowledging the founding principles on which Coco based her vision, he was also known to have quoted the words of the German writer and poet Goethe: "Make a better future by developing elements from the past".

The intention was to reinvent Chanel, and when Lagerfeld made his debut in the early 1980s he took the staple pieces – the tweed suit, the rope of pearls, the quilted bag, the cap-toe shoes – and manipulated the elements before representing them in a sensational way that may have surprised the purists. Early on he showed a succession of beautiful black evening dresses that took motifs directly from the Coromandel screens which decorated all of Chanel's homes. The dresses, which combined a 1920s drop-waist style with a more fitted body-conscious silhouette, were covered in lavish embroidery and delicate beading in the form of exotic camellia, foliage and oriental symbols: pure Coco with a King Karl twist. The iconic "Little Black Dress" that was so quintessentially Coco has remained a constant in the modern era, with Lagerfeld unleashing new ideas like fireworks: chiffon, lace, layers of tulle, embroidery and sequins, all to match the spirit of the times. Then he dipped into Coco's details to

"One is never over-dressed or underdressed with a Little Black Dress."

Karl Lagerfeld

define the look: strings of giant pearls, ropes of chainmail, crisp white contrasts in the collar and cuffs, or a perfectly placed camellia. Lagerfeld took his bow at the end of his 2005 autumn/winter prêt-à-porter collection, surrounded by models wearing updated interpretations of the versatile LBD.

While Coco reappropriated items of menswear and sporting uniforms for her collections, Lagerfeld also looked elsewhere, taking inspiration from the dress codes and unique styling details of urban sub-cults. For spring/summer 1991 Lagerfeld took Chanel to Californian surf school. His body-conscious sequinned jackets in vibrant primary colours were matched with black Lycra running shorts and sunglasses, and instead of the ubiquitous designer handbag the girls strolled down the catwalk with the ultimate beach accessory: a surfboard emblazoned with the double-C logo.

For autumn/winter 1992–93 he contrasted the toughness of the heavy biker boys uniform with the tenderness of a floaty ballerina skirt. Boxy black leather jackets with chunky gilt buttons and quilted sleeves were juxtaposed with pretty pastel evening gowns that fell to the floor in soft folds. Flat biker boots, leather caps and an overload of gilt chains hung from the neck, the waist and the wrists. While not readily identifiable as typical Chanel (understated simplicity) each new collection keeps enough traces of the trademark signatures (buttons with the double-C insignia, the iconic quilting, the camellia, the gilt chains) that allowed the house to progress in a modern idiom, assuring them of commercial success.

Lagerfeld was driven by curiosity for change, and was never unduly reverential in his role; as he said, "Absolute respect would have been fatal to creativity." The double-C insignia has adorned everything from high-top trainers to bra tops, Wellington boots and hot pants, and while

Previous pages Lagerfeld takes to the catwalk surrounded by models, all showing a variation on the versatile Little Black Dress, from autumn/winter 2005–6.

Left Knee-length leather biker boots get a Chanel makeover with the addition of the double-C logo, stamped in metal on the toecap.

Opposite Lagerfeld's inventive imagination allowed him to endlessly reinvent the Chanel suit without losing its original identity. His sketches show detailed variations on proportions and a wide range of fabric samples, from pastel tweeds, to leather.

Left A Chanel Boutique suit from the 1980s, made from green bouclé wool with black silk trim on the jacket collar, cuffs and pocket flaps. The single-breasted jacket has gilt buttons embossed with the double-C logo.

Opposite Bright red bouclé wool suit from 1983, the year Lagerfeld produced his first collection for the House of Chanel. The fitted jacket, with rows of gilt buttons and chain belt, together with the quilted cuff bracelet, take the iconography of Coco and re-present them as classic 1980s power dressing.

these things may be conceived as sensationalist elements designed to grab the headlines, it is still the Chanel suit that remains paramount to each collection, a re-imagined version of which will always be first down the catwalk.

During his tenure Lagerfeld upended the traditional twice-yearly fashion shows, a fixture of the house since the early 1930s. Tapping into a new age of social media, celebrity culture and an unparallel appetite for innovative imagery, Chanel now produce up to five shows each year, which by 2018 turned the company into a $10 billion luxury brand. With his impeccable sense of the cultural zeitgeist, and an inexhaustible compass of ideas, Lagerfeld created contemporary fashion that referenced technology, politics, humour as well as old-fashioned glamour, while still embracing the signature codes of Gabrielle Chanel.

Left A 1980s textured dress for the Chanel Boutique, printed with large cream polka-dots on black silk. The bodice is loosely cut with large pleats down the front, while the skirt has two pockets with gilt buttons embossed with the double-C insignia.

Opposite This advertising still for the Chanel Boutique, dating from the 1980s, was placed in magazines for the British market.

CHANEL

CHANEL
BOUTIQUE

26 OLD BOND STREET – LONDON W1

Above The black strapless bodice in silk organza flares out into a white knee-length skirt, with appliquéd "piano keys" at the hem. The dress, from 1985, has a ribbon sash with a camellia at the centre back.

Opposite Canadian supermodel Linda Evangelista wears a white sequinned sheath dress with dramatic black bows and black accessories for Chanel's spring/summer 1987 collection.

Above Black crepe coat-dress, edged in white rickrack braiding on the collar, cuffs and pockets and with Chanel cameo buttons, is an example of absolute elegance in monochrome, circa 1990.

Opposite Lagerfeld often combined wit with creativity to come up with his most surprising ideas, like this sporty sequinned surfer jacket with a zip-up fastening from the spring/ summer 1991 collection.

Opposite Linda Evangelista on the catwalk for spring/summer 1993. The abundance of jewellery and feather headdress create the spectacle, but the skills of couture are evident in the detailed flower embroidery decorating the simple grey tunic dress.

Right Suit proportions taken to extreme lengths for autumn/winter 1990–1. Model Yasmeen Ghauri wears a floor-length fitted coat with elaborate buttons and jewelled belt, with a gold lamé lining, over a short dark pink wool dress. On her wrists are the updated versions of the "mosaique" gold and jewelled bangles that Chanel used to wear.

Overleaf left A 2005 double-breasted trench coat in soft cotton becomes instantly recognizable as a Chanel trench when Lagerfeld adds contrasting braid to the front opening, shoulder seams, pockets, collar, belt and cuff edges.

Overleaf right Traditional tropes of the tweed suit, in a black and white colour palette, complete with braided trim and practical pockets, gets a high-tech update, accessorized with Stormtrooper helmet, plastic VR headsets and fembot-style gloves and Wellington boots in 2016.

Opposite Chanel's signature
jacket and staple use of tweed are
reinterpreted in 2011. Lagerfeld was
a master of reinvention with fabrics
beautifully deconstructed, jackets
resized to new proportions, and
multiple layering. Masculine trousers
were a mainstay of this collection
worn with clumpy workman's boots.

Above At the autumn/winter 2014
catwalk show, models strolled
the supermarket aisles as a nod to
consumer society. Wearing sweetie
necklaces and beautifully tailored
tweed tracksuits, psychedelic
iridescent trainers, with a classic
Chanel handbag reinvented as a
supermarket shopping basket.

Accessories

Coco's unique style was always to champion what was of her own making: comfortable clothes devoid of decoration, short hair because it was easier to deal with, and costume jewellery because she found real gems ostentatious. In truth, the foundations of so many of her groundbreaking and original ideas can be traced back to her own desire to enhance women's lives in a practical and simplistic way that erred on classicism, never exaggeration.

From the beginning, Coco excelled in putting together a complete look. Later on, her repetitive use of the same accessories (bag, shoes, gold chains, pearls, camellia) visually provided a Chanel trademark that came to define the house style. The famous quilted handbag, made to be worn rather than carried, was born out of frustration – Chanel herself was always losing the bag she carried. The elegant shoes with a tiny heel and a black toe-cap were invented to trick the eye into seeing the foot as smaller than it really was; her love of pearls was entirely based on a belief that they could enhance the beauty of any woman by highlighting sun-tanned skin and capturing the light of sparkling eyes.

Today, women who cannot afford to buy a Chanel suit, choose Chanel's covetable accessories instead. These provide a more affordable and realistic way for a larger audience to buy into a brand that speaks volumes in the world of fashion.

Opposite The timeless vision of Gabrielle Chanel, as she will always be remembered, in a simple black dress adorned with jewellery. The pearl necklaces, which she was rarely photographed without, became as identifiable with her style as the Little Black Dress.

Left A black and white diamond Camellia brooch, attached to a five-strand pearl choker necklace, was shown at the Chanel Madison Avenue Boutique, New York, in September 2010.

Opposite A vision in white, catwalk model Natalia Vodianova wears strings of pearl and white bead necklaces, with feather flowers in her hair, for the spring/summer 2003 collection.

Jewellery

Chanel was, of course, a woman of impossible contradictions, and while she advocated the trend for extravagant paste, she herself was always loaded with the real thing, usually bestowed on her by an abundance of wealthy boyfriends. Her lover, the Grand Duke Dmitri Pavlovich, escaped the Russian Revolution with a string of Romanov pearls that he gave to Coco, and which she then copied for her customers, thus starting the trend for fake pearls. The Duke of Westminster also gave her fabulous jewels, initially to woo her, and then later to make amends for his regular infidelities.

Coco was rarely seen without her jewellery; she usually combined pieces from her own collection with the presents she received from the men in her life, and her ropes of pearls became something of a trademark. The luminosity of pearls captured the light, she felt, and gave a flattering glow to the skin and eyes. Like much that she did to democratize fashion, jewellery was not to be saved for impressive occasions. She made it contemporary and wore it casually and without grandeur, at the beach or slung over her tweeds to go hunting.

In November 1932 she surprised everyone with an invitation
to view an exhibition of exquisite diamond jewellery that she had
designed. At a time of financial depression, it was a controversial
decision to work with priceless diamonds, taken by a woman who had
previously shunned precious stones. But thousands came to her private
rooms at Rue du Faubourg Saint-Honoré to look at Chanel's "Bijoux de
Diamants", trailing past the glass cases that were guarded by policemen
and which contained stunning pieces based on three main themes:
knots, stars and feathers. The spectacular diamonds were estimated at
the time to be worth 93 million francs! Lack of clasps and discreet
mounts made the elaborate pieces cleverly interchangeable – a brooch
could be worn as a hair ornament while a sunburst tiara could double
up as a necklace. Two of the most memorable pieces from 1932 have
recently been reissued: in 2007 the "Comète" necklace, made from

Opposite Chanel surprised
everyone with her "Bijoux de
Diamants" collection, which went
on show from her own apartment
in Paris in November 1932. This
diamond necklace with ribbon
bow mirrored Chanel's continual
use of the motif throughout her
long career.

Above The famous "Comète"
diamond necklace, originally
designed in 1932, was reissued
in 2007 as a classic piece of
jewellery. The necklace has no
clasps or clips and is simply placed
at the nape of the neck, with
the diamond trail sitting on the
opposite shoulder.

CHANEL

Above Based on the success of
the original "Comète" collection
(see previous page), new pieces
have been designed using similar
themes. This double-star ring and
ear-studs, made from white gold
and diamonds, is here shown in an
advertising still for Chanel in 2001.

Opposite The Italian Duke, Fulco
di Verdura, seen here with Chanel
in Paris in 1937, designed some
of her most memorable pieces
of jewellery, including the baked
enamel cuff, decorated with
coloured stones in the form of
the eight-point Maltese cross.

649 diamonds, sat like a collar around the neck, a shooting star placed on the collarbone with a cascading vapour trail designed to sit over the other shoulder; and the "Franges" bracelet, likewise inspired by the heavens, which had long diamond threads that fell over the hand.

These pieces she designed with Paul Iribe, an ambitious illustrator who was friends with Poiret and Cocteau, and with whom Coco had a serious romantic liaison, but he was not the only man to collaborate on her jewellery collections. For a short time she employed Count Étienne de Beaumont, and then another aristocrat, a Sicilian called Fulco Santo Stefano della Cerda, Duke of Verdura. The artistic Duke had originally wanted to become a painter, and had already worked with Coco as a textile designer before moving on to jewellery. Much of Chanel's most memorable work came from her collaboration with Verdura; they both shunned the boring "solitaire" rings that were popular at the time and instead took inspiration from the past. Verdura pioneered the revival of baked enamel, and taking motifs from medieval history he designed chunky bracelets that were studded with huge coloured stones in the form of the eight-pointed Maltese cross. The distinctive black-and-white cuffs became one of the most popular designs for Chanel; they were produced in many variations and Coco regularly wore one on each wrist. From 1924 onwards Chanel called on the expertise of an atelier called Maison Gripoix to execute her jewellery designs, using their skill with poured glass to create the boldly coloured baroque stones she loved. When Chanel relaunched in 1954 a young goldsmith called Robert Goosens developed the fashion for large pieces of artificial costume jewellery, which combined glass stones and pearls in a faux Renaissance gilt setting. Today the Goosens atelier has been bought out by the House of Chanel and continues to create exclusive handmade jewellery for them.

Opposite Chanel's signature use of pearls is taken to extremes in the early 1990s with this oversized choker, ropes of bracelets and large clip-on flower earrings made from pearls. Hanging from the neck is an outsize gilt cross, decorated with coloured glass and drop pearls. Yasmeen Ghauri was the face of Chanel, and the photograph was shot by Karl Lagerfeld.

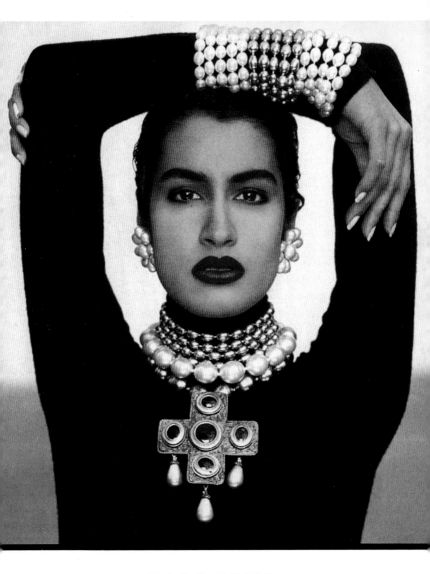

CHANEL
BOUTIQUE

26 OLD BOND STREET · LONDON W1   31 SLOANE STREET · LONDON SW1

The Chanel 2.55

In an era where a designer handbag has become the status symbol of a couture house, flaunted as a statement of wealth rather than taste, it is gratifying to find the original designer handbag still solidly aligned with the principles of its creator.

The Chanel handbag, like so much of Coco's fashion legacy, has become an instantly recognizable component of her iconography. The classic "2.55" was not the first bag Chanel produced – those came earlier in the 1930s – but it is the bag that has come to signify so much of Chanel's design philosophy within a single product. In much the same way that Coco used a number for her famous perfume, this bag was given a numerical name, which was derived from the month and year in which it was launched, February 1955. At a time when bags were usually held like a clutch, this was a new invention: designed to be worn over the shoulder rather than simply carried in the hands. The connection between Coco and her endlessly inventive design process can always be traced back to her own desire for simplicity and practicality. For her personal use she needed a bag that she wouldn't keep losing, so she added a shoulder strap, which left her hands free; she also wanted something that contained different compartments to hold her keys and cigarettes, so she conceived the idea of an inside pocket, a back flap, as well as a specific pocket for her lipstick so she would always have it to hand.

Left Designed by Chanel in 1955 for practical reasons – she was "weary of carrying my bags in my hand and losing them", this 1960s version of the famous 2.55 handbag remains true to the original design.

Opposite The overstitched quilted leather, chain shoulder strap and twist "Mademoiselle" lock are identifiable design details of the 2.55. This version is from 2005.

For the autumn/winter 1955 collection Chanel made two versions of her 2.55 bag, one intended for daywear, constructed from soft lambskin leather, which was strong but supple, and an evening version made from silk jersey. The distinctive Chanel quilting, or *matelassé*, was created by diamond-shaped top-stitching, meticulously sewn on top of the fabric and thought to have originated from the quilted fabric worn by the young stable lads that Coco met when she learnt to ride at Étienne Balsan's estate. The final component part was the metal chain woven through with leather, which may also have come from her memories of early days in the stables, as the juxtaposition of leather and metal is closely reminiscent of bridles and harnesses. There was an alternative metal strap made from flattened oval links (similar to the chains she used on the hems of her jackets to ensure they hung correctly). Both had visual and practical merits, and were strong enough to turn a handbag into an item that was wearable and useful. The front clasp was not adorned with the double-C insignia; instead it was a twist lock called the "Mademoiselle Lock".

Karl Lagerfeld reissued the bag in February 2005, as a commemorative product to celebrate the fiftieth anniversary of its debut, and has since continued to reinvent the 2.55 for each collection. Fabrics may be more inventive, colours more exotic, and dimensions deliberately extreme, but attention to detail never wavers. The Chanel signature turnlock closure and ID card with a unique number placed inside an interior pocket both guarantee the authenticity of each individual handbag.

Right Czech model Karolina Kurkova, in a British advertising campaign from 2004, carries a bright pink quilted leather tote bag. Lagerfeld often parodies the Chanel insignia, subverting and reinventing, as here where the discreet double-C logo is blown up to exaggerated proportions.

Opposite A witty reinvention of
the iconic chains used for belts
and handbag straps by Chanel,
Lagerfeld here embroiders multiple
chunky chains in a trompe-l'oeil
style onto black suede evening
gloves and a black jersey dress.
Worn with gold earrings, a large
gold chain necklace and gilt
buttons on the dress front, the
excessive theme from 1985 is
indicative of the era.

Above A fine gold chain belt
comprised of different sizes
and types of decorative chain
features the double-C insignia
on the fastening.

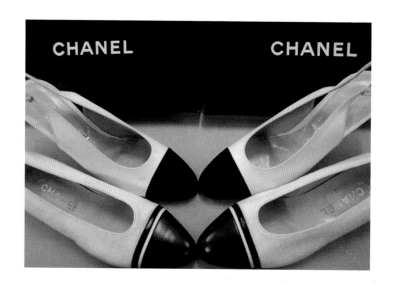

Shoes

There are pictures of Coco from as early as 1929 wearing flat shoes with a dark band across the toe and a neat little strap across the foot. Although she is unlikely to have designed this particular shoe herself, she went on to make the two-tone shoe her own. The first and now classic of these, which appeared in 1957, was very simple, elegant and comfortable to wear. Made by the house shoemaker, Monsieur Massaro, in nude leather to complement skin tone and visually elongate the length of the leg, the slingback slipper had very fine straps and a rounded black toe-cap that cleverly foreshortened the length of the foot. On a practical note, Coco was also aware that a shoe made entirely from pale leather would show every mark, and the invention of the dark toe would help to hide the odd dirty scuff!

Opposite top The classic two-tone cap-toe slingback style, with a small kitten heel, was the prototype for endless variations, like these flat ballet pumps with a thin red leather stripe.

Opposite bottom Lagerfeld has extended the Chanel shoe range to include every type of footwear, from jelly flip-flops to après-ski moon boots. These elegant slingbacks, made in soft black suede with crossover straps, date from the 1995 collection.

Right British model Karen Elson advertising Chanel shoes in a magazine campaign in 2006.

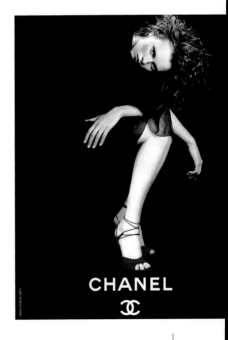

CHANEL

Beauty & Fragrance

"...that is what I was waiting for. A perfume like nothing else. A woman's perfume, with the scent of a woman"

Coco Chanel, on *Chanel No.5*

Chanel No. 5 is the most famous perfume in the world, and it remains the greatest success in the ongoing story of a woman determined to leave her mark on the twentieth century. Coco loved perfume and had an exceptional sense of smell – she often quoted the poet Paul Valéry: "A woman who doesn't wear perfume has no future"– and so it's surprising she waited until she was nearly 40 to launch her own fragrance in 1921.

Chanel was not the first couturier to diversify into the market, but unlike the others, who relied on romantic flower potions, she was the first to create a secret cocktail of more than 80 natural and synthetic ingredients, and then present it in a minimalist pharmaceutical-type bottle labelled only with her name and lucky number. The original formula was created by Ernest Beaux, an eminent French perfumier. He had a factory in Grasse where Coco spent many days suggesting different combinations of ingredients until she was finally presented with a series of miniature vials to test, labelled Nos. 1–24; Coco settled on bottle No. 5. There has always been speculation about the significance of the name (some say it came from her astrological sign, Leo, the fifth in the zodiac), but it is most likely she chose this clinical name to set herself apart from her competitors, who were marketing floral scents with evocative names. Beaux expressed his fear that with so many ingredients, jasmine being the most prominent but also neroli, ylang-ylang, sandalwood and May

Left The first advertisement for *Chanel No. 5*, circa 1924, featured the image of the designer herself. Typical of the Chanel ethos and the machine-age ideals of modernism, the name itself was abstract, the bottle square-cut and masculine, and the design and advertisements lacked the usual flourishes and flowers associated with perfume.

rose, the perfume would be very expensive. Without hesitation Coco declared: "I want to make the most expensive perfume in the world."

She took the samples back to Paris, atomised the shop and fitting rooms with the scent, gave tester vials to her best customers, and almost immediately found she had hit upon a winning formula. The perfume sold from the shops in Rue Cambon, Deauville, Biarritz and Cannes, but Coco, always adept at grabbing the opportune moment, wanted more. She approached Théophile Bader, the owner of Galeries Lafayette, with the idea that he should sell her perfume in his department store. Knowing that he would require greater quantities of stock than Ernest Beaux could produce, Bader introduced Coco to Pierre and Paul Wertheimer, a meeting that was to result in a lifelong business association that changed all their lives. The brothers, who owned one of France's largest cosmetic and fragrance companies, Les Parfumeries Bourjois, agreed to fully finance production, distribution and marketing for all her beauty products, and in 1924 they set up a company called Les Parfums Chanel, giving Coco just ten per cent of the company. It was a decision she came to regret, as the profits from the business that bore her name escalated into millions, but despite many legal wrangles over the years, the Wertheimers (who to this day have kept Chanel in private ownership) were reliable business partners, and ultimately responsible for the vast wealth that allowed Coco to be financially secure and to live independently.

Ernest Beaux invented new fragrances for Chanel – *Cuir de Russie* (1924), *Bois des Îles* (1926) and *Gardenia* (1927) – but they were never to equal the success of *No. 5*, which came to be associated with the most beautiful women in the world. Other fragrances included the first men's cologne *Pour Monsieur*, in 1955, and in 1970, just before Chanel's death, *No. 19*, which was aimed at a younger audience. The "nose" behind the House of Chanel today is Jacques Polge, who has continued to expand the line with many new fragrances including *Allure* (1996), *Coco Mademoiselle* (2001) and *Chance Eau Tendre* (2010).

Right By 2001, *Chanel No. 5* was seen as a symbol of idealized womanhood and advertised by visuals that linger on the glamour and beauty of Hollywood. In most of the ads, the bottle is transparent, in line with the original concept of the "invisible" bottle.

Left *Chance* was developed by Jacques Polge in 2002. The perfume is light, bright and floral with notes of jasmine and citrus fruit.

Right Clean and zingy with a hint of spice, musk and cedarwood, *Egoiste Platinum* launched in 1993, after the phenomenal success of the original male fragrance *Egoiste*.

ÉGOÏSTE
PLATINUM

CHANEL

Cosmetics & Skincare

Coco adored make-up: she thought it pretentious to leave the house barefaced, and was rarely seen without charcoal eyes and a slash of vermilion across the mouth. In 1924 she made an early blood-red lipstick for herself. Encased in a mother-of-pearl tube, this went on to become the prototype for countless shades of Chanel red lipstick. As with her instinctive requirements for functional clothes, her own beauty needs influenced her commercial products. From 1930 onwards, Coco produced an expanding range of beauty products including face powders, moisturizing oils, perfumed talcum powder and oil for sunbathing. All these products were marketed in ultra-modern black cases, with chic black-and-white packaging stamped with the double-C logo. Today the black packaging of the brand is instantly recognizable around the world as the creative team at Chanel combine scientific innovation with cutting-edge technology to produce a flawless range of beauty products. The house legacy remains intact: to provide women with products that enhance natural beauty and also cultivate individual differences, with the ultimate aim of being as unique as Coco.

EXTRAIT DE ROUGE
CHANEL

Left A magazine advert for classic red lipstick Rouge Extreme, 1997. Coco Chanel was never seen without her trademark vermilion red lips, and the legacy remains today with endless shades of rouge created for each new collection.

Opposite Chanel began the bodycare range with the launch of perfumed soap for the "toilet and the bath", infused with the fragrance of *Chanel No. 5*, the most famous perfume in the world, seen here in a 1940s advertisement.

IN PURSUIT OF *Loveliness*

For the perfectionist who must be exquisitely groomed from head to toe...Chanel soaps for the toilet and bath...breathing the fragrance of the most famous perfumes in the world.

Toilet Soap, perfumed with No. 5...3 in box, $3.00 · Hand Soap, perfumed with Gardenia...
4 in box, $2.00 · Bath Soap, perfumed with Gardenia...1 in box, $1.50 · Chanel Perfumes
...No. 5, Gardenia, Russia Leather, Glamour, No. 22...$2.75 to $25.50 · *All prices plus tax*

by **CHANEL**

No. 5, No. 22, Glamour Reg. U. S. Pat. Off. Chanel, Inc., N. Y. Distributors

Resources

Baudot, Francois, *Chanel: Fashion Memoir*, Thames and Hudson, 1996.

Bott, Daniele, *Chanel: Collections and Creations,* Thames and Hudson, 2007.

Charles-Roux, Edmonde, *Chanel and Her World*, Weidenfeld and Nicolson, 1982.

De La Haye, Amy, Tobin, Shelley, *Chanel: The Couturière at Work*, V&A Publications, 1994.

Madsen, Axel, *Coco Chanel: A Biography*, Bloomsbury, 1990.

Morand, Paul, *The Allure of Chanel*, Pushkin Press, 2008.

Picardie, Justine, *Coco Chanel: The Legend and the Life*, Harper Collins, 2011.

Wallach, Janet, *Chanel: Her Style and Her Life*, Mitchell Beazley, 1999.

Index

Acknowledgments

Author's Acknowledgements

Thanks go to the superb collections from the Victoria & Albert Museum, the Arizona Costume Institute at the Phoenix Art Museum, Kerry Taylor Auctions, and to Clare Hutton for her invaluable research. Special thanks to my fabulous editor Lisa Dyer and all the team at Carlton Books.

Picture Credits

Howie: 124, /Gift of Mrs. Wesson Seyburn, Photo by Ken Howie: 32
Photo 12: /Wolf Tracer Archive: 63
Réunion des Musées Nationaux: /©BnF, Dist. RMN /Séeberger Collection: 17, /
Ministère de la Culture-Médiathèque du Patrimoine, Dist. RMN: 64
Shuterstock: 126, 127 /The Art Archive: /Collection Dagli Orti: 138, /
The Kobal Collection: /Goldwyn /United Artists: 61
Sharok Hatami: 85, 91, 95, 97, 99, 100, 101, /Marco Madeira/
Moviestore Collection: 62, /Geoff Wilkinson: 112
Topfoto.co.uk: 3, 74, 102, /The Granger Collection: 1, 6, 16, 46, /
Roger Viollet: 11, 24, 52, 82l, 84, 115, 135, /Roger Viollet /R.Briant
et L.Degrâces / Galliera: 42, 43, /Roger Viollet /R.Briant et P. Ladet/
Galliera: 27, /Roger Viollet / L.Degrâces et P.Ladet / Galliera: 38, /
Roger Viollet /Phillipe Ladet et Claire Pignol /Galliera: 29, /Roger
Viollet /Musée Carnavalet: 146, /Ullsteinbild: 98, 132, 133
Victoria & Albert Museum/V&A Images – All rights Reserved: 23, 31,
69l, 79, 81, 118, 121, 125, 144b

Every effort has been made to acknowledge correctly and contact
the source and/or copyright holder of each picture and Welbeck
Publishing apologizes for any unintentional errors or omissions,
which will be, corrected in future editions of this book.

Page 1 *Portrait of Mademoiselle Chanel,* 1923, by Marie Laurencin. Chanel commissioned the portrait when the pair met working for the Ballets Russes, but then turned down the finished portrait as she did not think it a fair representation.

Page 2 Detail from Chanel spring/summer 2007 ready-to-wear collection by Karl Lagerfeld, with diamond Coco brooch and camellia cuff bracelet.

Overleaf Illustration of a Chanel dress by Jean Cocteau 1939, with red, white and blue cornflowers and poppies on the bodice.